Please Hear My Cry

Silent Abuse at the Hands of a Christian Narcissist

Sharon L. Johnson

BK Royston Publishing
P. O. Box 4321
Jeffersonville, IN 47131
502-802-5385
http://www.bkroystonpublishing.com
bkroystonpublishing@gmail.com

© Copyright – 2020

All Rights Reserved. No part of this book may be reproduced, stored in a retrieval system, or transmitted by any means without the written permission of the author.

Cover Design: Gad of Elite Book Covers

ISBN-13: 978-1-951941-32-1

Bible King James Version – Public Domain

Printed in the United States of America

Dedication

This book is dedicated to my mother; my best friend, my covering, my pillar and my rock in many of my trying times. Thank you so much for teaching me how to be a strong woman while on my Christian journey and while overcoming much adversity.

I also dedicate this book to all the strong women out there - Pastor Wives, Women in all levels of Leadership within ministry and to all of my precious sisters that may be just starting out or going through their spiritual journey in this season. But maybe they are dealing with silent abuse or coming out of silent abuse in this season and they are afraid, ashamed, silent and feeling as if they are alone. I share my story, to let you know that you are not alone. I was in a silently abusive marriage for many years. It was if it I had become paralyzed, fearful, ashamed, quiet, and so drained to the place, where I felt as if life was literally being sucked right out of me. While also feeling as if, no one would understand, because I was the only one going through this. Silent abuse is real and it comes in many forms. This abuse can affect you very negatively, naturally and spiritually even more so if in its long-term state you do not have the Lord's help. Let me reassure you of something, that no it wasn't you; you are not crazy and the silent abuse that you went through, was never warranted and you did not deserve it. I want to encourage you and let you know that I am a survivor of silent abuse. God allowed me to live, to tell you my story of how the enemy tried to use silent abuse against me and my purpose, but how God is going to use it for His Godly purpose. Every one of you are survivors. God wants to use your individual stories for His glory in this season. It's your time to ARISE, no more shame and no more SILENCE!!!

Acknowledgements

I first acknowledge Jesus Christ, my Lord and Savior for giving me the idea to write my first book. So grateful unto him for the necessary gifts he had placed on the inside of me to be able to birth this book. I thank him for the courage and strength that was needed for me to relive my past, while putting it in book form. I thank him for being my main accountability partner and for giving me the much needed encouragement, the push, persistence, focus and discipline to get this project completed. I love him so much and he will get all the glory and from this book.

To my deceased parents, my mother, Nannie M. Johnson, my mentor, my encourager, my example, my spiritual and my natural mom, who knew the right thing to say, always at the right time; that always left me encouraged. My father, Willis Johnson, for being there and loving on me. To the both, who always supported me and were my biggest encouragers and supporters, in whatever I set out to do.

I thank God for the special circle of friend(s), that he placed around me during this time. Tina

Riley, Delores Drummond, Emma Williams, Sylvia Richardson and Sandra McAllister who have been my encouragement, accountability partners, prayer partners, who kept me and the book covered in prayer and who were also my prophetic voices, who spoke constant life in me and over the book, throughout this entire process. Each one of them, have been such a blessing to me in this season, and I am so grateful and I love them so much.

Table of Contents

Dedication	iii
Acknowledgement	v
Introduction	xi
Innocent Beginnings	1
Turned Up Pursuit	11
The Set-Up	17
Why Did He Marry Me?	29
Go Through Season	41
Pursued In Love Or Lust?	43
I Was In A Competition	45
Silent Abuse	47
Unequally Yoked	51
Who Was I In Covenant With?	53

Master Manipulator	59
Financial Woes	61
Christian Narcissist?	63
Public Face/Private Face	77
False Prophet	85
Satan's Plots Against Godly Covenants	93
The Aftermath	95
Demonic Warfare-It's A Family Thing	103
Manifestation Time- The Real Deal	107
God's Will Be Done	115
No Support	123
Desert Season	125
Healing Process Begins	127
Effect On The Children	131

Closing	135
Encouragement	137
Conclusion And Encouragement	139
End Testimony	143
Closing Remarks	145
End Of Story	147

Introduction

I am so grateful to God for allowing me this awesome opportunity to write my first book. It's the story about my Christian journey and how many wrong choices and decisions I made early in my walk landed me in covenant with the wrong one. This relationship almost took my destiny and my life!

These wrong choices came with much disappointment, abuse, manipulation, control, shame, devalue, disrespect, betrayal, and deception from the hands of my covenant partner of 35 years. Yes, he had the church titles, he dressed the part, he talked the talk and was very well versed in the Word of God. He wore the mask of a believer and went through the motions of pretending as if he really loved and feared the Lord. "Having a form of Godliness but denying the power thereof from such turn away." (2 Timothy 3:5) (ESV). He had it all together on the outside, spiritually, but nothing at all about his heart resembled God. "Because this people draw near with their mouth and honor me with their lips, while their hearts are far from me, and their fear of me is a commandment taught by men." (Isaiah 29:13) (ESV)

I will be transparent and share how I innocently gave this individual, who had no apparent identity, access into my life, space, and heart. He came with no expectations for his own life and surely had little or no expectations for me or both of our lives together. In the beginning, his empty love seemed real with promises he made, and the things he would do for me without me even asking. However, I found out later and confirmed down the road, it was not real love. They were only fake empty promises he made all laced with his definition of false toxic love.

Of course, now that I am out of it, I wonder how I so quickly and innocently allowed myself to fall for the lies of a person who was very broken, insecure, deceptive, and toxic. This individual made me feel less than my worth and accept less than what I really deserved in life. I lost precious time.

I will share how it was only because of God's love, protection, sustaining power, strength, and help that He victoriously brought me through and eventually out of a toxic union. It was a union filled with silent abuse from the hands of a masked non-believer who unfortunately carried the title of my husband. "Beware of false prophets. They come to you disguised as sheep, but in their hearts they are vicious wolves." (Matthew 7:15) (GWT) He was clearly being used by the enemy to try to kill me and everything inside of me that resembled God and my identity in God. "The thief cometh not, but for to steal and to kill and to destroy." (John 10:10) (KJV).

I wrote this book, unscathed, in my right mind, and I still don't even look like what I've been through. I'm s-o-o-o grateful unto the Lord for His faithfulness. Although, towards the end, I felt as if I was in a war zone and sleeping with the enemy; yes, the very one held me tight and laid next to me in bed every night. I'm sharing my story to help someone who may have gone through a similar relationship or is going through it right now. Don't give up if you are confused and don't know what's next. This book will give you encouragement and let you know nothing is happening in our lives that catches God by surprise. It may surprise us but not Him. He only wants what's best for us. Sometimes very hurtful and devastating things happen to free us and for our story to be used for God's glory.

There are many people like me, who are either in it, going through it, or either coming out of it but are ashamed and don't want anyone to know what's happening for multiple reasons. Someone may be in a relationship with a very prominent or upcoming figure in the church and/or community and don't want to expose how shameful and badly they are or have been treated by the person. They may want to save the abuser's name because, and don't want to break a church up, especially if it's the Pastor/Bishop/Apostle. Some may feel as if they have too much history or time invested in the relationship and/or have a fear of starting all over by themselves. So many people just maintain their position so they can at least tell everyone, "Well, we've had some hard times, but at least we are still married." While they remain silent and hold back, they wear a smile and live abused, lonely, and miserable lives at the hands of church and community leaders.

Whatever your reason may be, remember God has given us all a purpose in life and in His

Kingdom. Just ask yourself this question, "Are you walking boldly and freely in your Kingdom purpose, or are you being held back by what you have attached or have allowed yourself to attach itself to you?" There is nothing worse than living an unsatisfied, unfulfilled life was full of silent abuse purposely sent by the enemy to stop your flow of being everything God had intended you to be. The result is an unfulfilled life while you were alive. You were filled with things the Lord put on the inside of you (purpose), but you never emptied out or walked in your purpose.

 I could be very ashamed of my story and not want to tell anyone about it. Instead, I chose to share it. I faced many challenges, much opposition, shame, disgrace, open disrespect, and attempted character assassination from the hands of my covenant partner. He made conscious and intentional decisions to publicly expose every private thing we were going through to the church, our family, and the community.

 I have been in church since the age of 6. Throughout all those years, the church kept this type of behavior silent. But I want to let my brothers and sisters know this silent abuse is boldly and frequently happening in the church at the hands of church leadership. Although it is being treated as a white elephant in the room and not being acknowledged or addressed because of the position and titles people hold within the church, I encourage you to be strong and not to be ashamed. You are not crazy, and you are not the only one going through or have gone through this type of silent abuse.

The silent abuse I was under for many years had begun to suck the life out of me naturally, spiritually, and emotionally. It was a very desperate and low time in my life, and no one knew it. Over the years, my situation continued to spiral down and eventually became a 911 emergency for every part of me. I sought God for direction, and to SAVE myself and my life, I had to leave my covenant.

There is absolutely nothing wrong with SAVING yourself from silent abuse within the church. There are others, like me, who have made it, and we are still standing because of God's loving help. Rest assured, there is no fear when you trust

God for real and give the entire situation to Him. He will never steer you wrong.

God wants us to live our best life. Don't give up, regardless of what caused your world to be turned upside down, seems like it has stopped turning, or all you feel is pain, despair, hopelessness, hurt, and brokenness in your life. Be encouraged and know this is not the end of your story. It's not over until God says it's over. It is only the beginning, and better days are ahead of you.

You are a survivor, and so am I! "Yet in all these things, we are more than conquerors through Him who loved us." (Romans 8:37). (NKJV) Be very encouraged and know that God is not finished with you, and He is going to take your hurt and pain and use it for His purpose! He will turn your misery into your ministry.

God healed me and put my life back together again, all the broken pieces of my heart, my emotions, and my soul. Regardless of how broken you may look or feel because life was so unfair to you and caused you to feel unworthy for God's use, He still needs you and wants to use you so mightily. Sometimes, God will reroute you on another path.

Be content with and know that He does have a plan for your life. "For I know the plans I have for you," declares the Lord, plans to prosper you and not to harm you, plans to give you hope and a future." (Jeremiah 29:11). (NIV) Be encouraged!

I pray each word from the front to the back of this book blesses, inspires, and encourages you. I pray it will also be a resource full of information. I pray you become more aware and understand the real importance of making sure God is in every piece of the equation when it comes to your asking, seeking, pursuing, and waiting on the right mate. Please consult God about everything in your life before you do anything, especially when it comes to covenant and relationship partners. "Trust in the Lord with all thine heart; and lean not unto thine own understanding. In all thy ways acknowledge him, and he shall direct thy paths." (Proverbs 3:5-6). (KJV)

Please Hear My Cry

Silent Abuse at the Hands of a Christian Narcissist

Innocent Beginning

This is a story about my life when I was in covenant with a masked non-believer who had the dress, had the talk, very well versed in the Word, and had the form of Godliness, down to a tee. "Woe unto you, scribes and Pharisees, hypocrites! For ye are like unto whited sepulchres, which indeed appear beautiful outward, but are within full of dead men's bones, and of all uncleanness." (Matthew 23:27) (KJV) This person was my husband, Deacon Todd. The relationship I had with him almost took my life and my spiritual destiny, all while we were in the church.

He was my first in everything. I had no idea my real first love relationship, or so I thought, would come in the form of everything else but real true love. He came with abuse, deception, competition with his fantasies, infidelity, shame, disrespect, toxic dysfunction, and repeated cycles of generational curses from his family's line. I had no idea his love would be so toxic and feel like daggers sent from him to intentionally puncture my heart every chance he could get.

Was there ever a time in your life when you were in a relationship that felt right? The right things were said, the right things were done, the chemistry was right, and you felt a love connection. You reminisced over all the things you were told, and all the promises made to you. But down the road, you found out it was all lies. They were all empty, false promises that meant absolutely nothing. For me, it was very apparent that it was a way for my husband to gain access to the open door of my innocent heart while firmly securing the key over the very thing which kept me alive. Once my heart was secured, and he had the key, that's when my love connection and the real world went totally in a bad, toxic direction.

I thought I had only allowed one person in my life, my space, and in my heart. That was false because I had also freely invited all those things attached to his past. At the time, I didn't understand any of this because I was young and in religion. I didn't have a relationship with God. Deacon Todd also brought unpacked baggage that contained all his brokenness, insecurities, childhood hurts, fatherless issues, abandonment, and rejection. In addition to all of this, there were his grandfather's/father's generational curses running through his bloodline that was never dealt with or ever broken off his life.

He was the person who made me feel good. He was the one who I felt was good to me but was not good for me. He was the person who I had allowed to occupy my space (my heart and my mind).

In the beginning, I didn't realize I had allowed a great pretender, a masked manipulator and controller, a false prophet, and a Christian narcissist to ensnare my heart and to silently abuse me. All the while, I was wasting so many precious years of my life.

The only reason I am still alive and standing strong is because of the grace, mercy, love, and the help of the Lord. My silent pain came from a person who was close to me but had a false perception of who he was and what he wanted and needed in life with me. His good intentions appeared to be honest and real on the outside, but on the inside, there were evil intentions, and nothing was honest or real about them at all. "Even so ye also outwardly appear righteous unto men, but within ye are full of hypocrisy and iniquity." (Matthew 23:28) (KJV)

Much of my silent pain came through him and his carnal and unsaved village of "yes" men and women in and outside of the church. This village respected and supported all his wrongdoings towards his covenant and his family. They did not make him accountable when they saw him doing wrong. During that time, I had asked one of his spiritual brothers in his village to help him before he destroyed his covenant and family. His response totally surprised me. He said, "Deacon Todd doesn't want to stop doing what he is doing." His village supported, respected, stroked, and reverenced him while not making him accountable for the wrong things he did. "But now I am writing to you that you must not associate with anyone who claims to be a brother or sister but is sexually immoral or greedy, an idolater or slanderer, a drunkard or swindler. Do not even eat with such people." (1 Corinthians 5:11) (NIV)

This silent pain came with much deception, disrespect, control, fraud, manipulation, public shame, disgrace, humiliation, rejection, lies, abandonment, abuse, and misuse. It did not come from one of my enemies who reproached me, or someone I knew who hated me. It was from my equal, my companion, my covering, and close friend. A person that said he loved me and said he loved the Lord. A man I shared innermost secrets with, fellowshipped with, walked in the church house together with, trusted, and had confidence in. "Now it is not an enemy who insults me; otherwise I could bear it; it is not a foe who rises up against me; otherwise I could hide from him. But it is you, a man who is my peer, my companion and good friend! We used to have close fellowship; we walked with the crowd into the house of God." (Psalms 55:12-14) (CSB). It came from a person on the outside who appeared to be all together, spiritually and acted as if they really loved God and the things of God. But was just a fictitious person full of deception and full of himself and was more concerned about impressing people than impressing God. I had given my heart and love to a masked unbeliever. He was broken, insecure, hurting, toxic and dysfunctional and kept producing a tainted and fake love, which only caused me pain, suffering, and misery. He knew how to give and do nice things, but it seemed as if he did not know how to genuinely love a person. This was Deacon Todd, and he was my husband.

  I was a very young, shy, and naive little girl who had accepted Christ in my life at a very young age. I had been in a religious church for most of my life and raised in a Christian home with a mother, father, and ten siblings including myself. Our family consisted of two sets of twins;

I had a twin sister, and the other twins were a boy and a girl. Our foundation was built as God had instructed. We were taught good morals and values and how to respect and treat people with loving-kindness and, most importantly, how to fear and reverence the Lord. "Train up a child in the way he should go, and when he is old, he will not depart from it." (Proverbs 22:6)

My mother was a Proverbs 31 woman who was an excellent example before all of us as to how a godly Christian woman and wife should act! My parents did an awesome job raising all ten of us. They completed their Godly assignment over our lives.

I was in my last year of high school and in a school/job program. Right after high school, the job landed me a full-time position at a Fortune 500 Company. I was still living with my parents, so I was financially set at that time. I wasn't a worldly girl and had no experience with things in the world like partying, clubbing, smoking, turning it up, etc. I had been raised in church most of my life, so, work and church were pretty much all I did, knew, and wanted to do.

I knew Deacon Todd from high school because we were in a typing class together. He was a year ahead of me and had already graduated before he expressed an interest in dating me. Now mind you, he and I really had nothing in common as I would soon find out. I wondered what it was about me that he found so attractive, especially with our lifestyles being so different. Humm. Through my youthful and naive eyes, the enemy had a plan, but I didn't see it. Deacon Todd seemed to be very experienced when it came to life itself. He had the gift of gab and was extremely easy to talk to. We talked about everything and anything, whether sports, politics, or religion.

He knew what to say and how to say it, and he always had an answer for everything, whether wrong or right. He came across as a noticeably confident individual with no insecurities or issues at all and appeared very well packaged on the outside. Deacon Todd was definitely caught up in his appearance and his material things and wasn't ashamed to brag on it. "People will be lovers of themselves, lovers of money, boastful, proud, abusive, disobedient to their parents, ungrateful, unholy." (2 Timothy 3:2) (NIV) I was totally the opposite; where material things didn't excite me at all. I was just flattered that he didn't look too bad, seemed like a nice guy, and he wanted to go on a date with me.

Side note of wisdom: There are many women out there who will size a guy up and decide if she wants him because of the material things he has, or she thinks he possesses on the outside. Please hear me, and don't be fooled by that. There is a good chance you are setting yourself up for heartache down the road if you are just looking at the outside of what a man appears to have or brings to the table.

While we were still in school, Deacon Todd set up a date a few times, but something always came up, so he never followed through on it. There was another time when he was supposed to come over to visit me at my parent's house, but he didn't make it. It was a real turn off to me. So, I phoned him that same night and told him I didn't want to date him anymore and let's end it. And we did. I didn't realize God was trying to end the relationship before it even got started. But "I" missed it (sigh).

Now mind you, back in the day I came up in, we weren't being taught relationships, covenants, and the importance of seeking then waiting on God for your right mate. Couples dated and married because they said they loved each other. Later down the road, some would go through the good and bad, mostly the bad. Couples did what they saw everyone else do to maintain and remain in dysfunctional and abusive marriages in the church. Many walked around with no physical marks of abuse for others to see. But they were walking around with a fractured heart and soul from constant trauma resulting from silent abuse endured in their homes from partners who were church leaders with a title.

    Years passed, and I was seeking more of God, although still in a religious church. Out of the blue, Deacon Todd called and told me he was in the Marine Corp and wanted to take me out on a date. So, what do you think I did? I gave him another chance. In my mind, I reasoned that he didn't seem like such a bad guy. I was talking with my twin about him and she said, "give him another chance, maybe the armed services have grown him up."

Sharon L. Johnson

Turned Up Pursuit

So, we started dating again while he was still in the service. At that point in the relationship, Deacon Todd didn't have Christ in his life, but I did. He knew what I stood for, so we were not sexually active at all. We just spent a lot of innocent time together when he came home on military leaves. We ate out, went to church, and to the movies, etc. In the beginning, he was so loving, kind, affectionate, and caring. We had the same mindset, which was that "We just wanted to spend as much time together as possible." He was so easy to talk with about anything and just made it more enjoyable. I just wanted to spend time with him.

Soon, our dating was in full swing. Deacon Todd captured my heart and my head, and he knew it. Now, it seemed as if the words out of his mouth were smooth as butter. They sounded true and promising and never caused me to think twice or even question what he was saying and judge it as accurate or not. Time passed on and I thought to myself, maybe he's the one, and the armed services had grown him up.

Further, into our relationship, his pursuit for me became even stronger. I was frequently told of his love for me. His words were so convincing, and his actions were so alluring. The time we spent together made me feel as if he was only attentive to me and my needs. He really made me feel as if we had a serious love connection going on for one another. His words were what every woman likes to hear from her man. He gave me anything I wanted and bought me things spontaneously to show he was thinking of me. He wanted me to be his wife and made all kinds of promises. We talked about the type of house we wanted and the neighborhood we wanted to live in. He said I would be taken care of and not need anything. It seemed so right. The crazy thing about all this is he did start out doing all the beautiful things, and it seemed to line up with all his words and promises.

Although we were only dating, he seemed to put into practice, Ephesians 5:25, in the beginning. Where it instructs the husbands to love your wives, just as Christ loved the church and gave himself up for her. He walked it out very well, early on in our relationship. He made and spent quality time with me. The respect he gave me and how he valued our relationship; while he put me above his friends. How he showed his concern for me; while he protected and covered me. The gentleness he showed me and how he seemed to be so focused only on me. How endlessly he complimented me. All of these things, of course, made me feel incredibly special and loved by him. I thought he was the one for me, and I was the one for him. I felt confident and secure with him in the love relationship we had together. The love between us appeared so real, secure, and able to endure whatever storms would come our way. It seemed as if we were pre-destined to walk out our Godly destinies together.

At this point, we had been dating for a while, and we were casually talking about marriage and our next steps. Around the same time, Deacon Todd began to send military allotments home for my own personal use "just because." I felt it was such a big and nice gesture on his part, especially since we were still only dating. Later on, down the road, to only find out that the kind gesture was only a set-up for a beginning of significant financial hardship for me. All that time, Deacon Todd carried himself in such a way and had a certain aura about himself that gave a vibe that he was the kindest person around and didn't have a bad bone in his body.

He had me. This young, green behind the ears church girl with little experience about the world, evil people in it, or what it offered was totally into this man. He had my heart and my head. I was exactly where he wanted me to be. I found out where he wanted me was in the palm of his hands to manipulate, control, and make me feel loved with empty, false love. When I love, I love hard, and I give of myself entirely, especially when the feeling is being reciprocated. He took full advantage of me sexually, financially, emotionally, as well as all my kindness.

Each time Deacon Todd came home on military leaves, it was so special. We both were always filled with anticipation and couldn't wait to see each other. We spent quality time together without sex. We acted as if we hadn't seen each other in years, although it had been a couple of months. It all seemed so real. But things began to change the more time we spent together. It became very smothering and unenjoyable. Deacon Todd began to act as if he owned me, and I was his property. He made me feel as though I owed him something for all the nice things he had done and was doing for me. His moves were always subtle, smooth, and strategic, which made it easy to miss because it came across like he was really into me and loved me. It was puzzling. It was all wrapped in his definition of love, which was empty and toxic. Although his love seemed a little off to me, it was noticeably clear he knew how to love himself. "People will be lovers of themselves." (2 Timothy 3:2) It finally got to the place where spending time with him was smothering me, and I wanted to give him some space. But the more I pushed away from him, the harder he worked to pull me closer. We continued to date, and I should have jumped ship, but I didn't. Although I was feeling uncomfortable in the relationship, Deacon Todd still had my head and heart. And he knew it.

On one of his leaves, I asked him to go to church with me. That Sunday, he accepted Jesus Christ in his life and got baptized in Jesus' Name. I was so excited for him. It seemed like he took the next step toward having a relationship with God. Of course, this caused me to shift my focus from his excessive smothering and the feeling like I was his property.

Sometime after his baptism, he proposed marriage to me, and I accepted. But the control, manipulation, and smothering spirit began to resurface, so I gave the engagement ring back. Yet, he still had my heart. He knew it too and just kept pursuing me even harder.

I know it sounds crazy, but despite the signs, he apologized, and we reconciled again. Although in my gut, I knew something wasn't right, but my head and heart had already settled in for the long run. I became blinded by his empty love.

The Set-Up

Deacon Todd is still in the Marine Corps; but we are engaged now. He comes home on another leave and wanted to spend some time together. Our relationship up to this point, did not consist of sex at all because of the boundaries that had been set early on in our relationship. He suggested that we go to his mother's house and give her a visit. I was in total agreement, because I loved his mom and enjoyed spending time with her and him together. When we get to his mother's house, there wasn't anyone home. So we proceed to the den area to relax, watch TV and so I thought, to wait on his mother's return.

At this point, I trusted him, I believed that he loved me, we were soon to be husband and wife, he had my heart and I didn't think that he would intentionally do anything to try and hurt me or my heart in any way. So, we are just enjoying one another's company and he ask something of me; that surprised me and seemed so innocent all at the same time. "Can I just place it in, I will not do anything in you?" Well, I believed him and foolishly allowed that request, why? because I had given him my heart and he knew it.

Well, next month comes around and I miss my cycle. I go to the doctor and he tells me that I am pregnant. My first reaction to the doctor's test result was complete silence. I then ask the question, "are you sure and could that test result be inaccurate"? He then proceeds to tell me how far along I was in weeks. When I left the doctor's office, my emotions and thoughts were all over the place. I cried ... I was devastated, I was hurt, I was upset, I was angry, I felt betrayed and LIED to; but my heart was still tied to him. I was in a very confused and unhappy place. I just had questions ... Why did he LIE to me? Why didn't he tell me that he had released in me? I thought he loved me? Why would he trick me? Why would he impregnate me before we were even married? Was this intentional? Was this a deliberate act to entrap me into making sure that I marry him? What was his motive behind all this?

After the dust settled and I got my emotions under control, I told Deacon Todd that I was pregnant and I ask him why did he do it; why didn't he tell me he had released in me and why had he been so dishonest to me? He smoothed right over with more lies in his calm soothing voice tone, while reassuring me that he would take care of me and take on his responsibilities and do the right thing by the child and me. He said, since we were already planning on getting married anyway, he would talk to my parents and explain everything.

He did speak with my parents and asked for my hand in marriage. However, my parents were reluctant and didn't want him to marry me because I was pregnant. He was very persuasive and adamant while making empty promises to them about how he was going to take very good care of their daughter and their grandbaby.

Why didn't I leave him and run for my life after all the dishonesty that manifested in him? Because I was in love with him and he had my heart and he knew it.

One wrong decision made in my life, continued to lead to others and before I knew it, my life was totally spiraling out of control and farther away from God's will for my life.

My story reminds me somewhat of King David and Bathsheba. David made the decision to lay with Bathsheba even though he knew she was married. When she announced her pregnancy, David gave a command to put her husband on the front-line to be killed, and then he married her. It was apparent David's actions were out of the temptations of sin, the lust of the flesh, lust of the eyes and the pride of life. Out of his own selfishness reasons, he wanted Bathsheba for himself, at whatever cost necessary. When I look at my story, Deacon Todd desired me, although he knew what I stood for, impregnated me upon deception, resulting in a quick unexpected wedding with an innocent baby on the way. One wrong decision kept leading to another wrong decision.

Wow! Because of temptations of sin, my life had taken another course of direction that surely wasn't the direction God had initially mapped out for me! And I would soon find out!

I definitely had been caught up in a lust move and not a love move. Wrong decisions have dire consequences, even the innocent ones can lead to many regrets. When people are tempted, temptation comes from the lure of their own desires. **Sin doesn't only affect the people involved in the act, it affects everyone who was innocently included in decisions down the road. Which can come in the form of a spiritual or natural death or generational curses.** "Then, when lust has conceived, it gives birth to sin, and when sin is accomplished, it brings forth death." (James 1:15) (NKJV)

Now all kinds of things are going on in my head. I thought Deacon Todd was really in love with me. Why wasn't he honest with me and tell me he had released and was only lusting after me? Even after all this, he had a way with words that always seemed so soothing and made me feel as if things were going to be okay regardless of whatever the situation was. You think I would have taken off running after finding out about the pregnancy, but I was deep in it then, and he had my heart and mind, and he knew it. My mindset shifted to the role of becoming a new mother and wife.

Side note: Real love doesn't lie to you; it doesn't hurt you, and it doesn't deceive you. "While evildoers and imposters will go from bad to worse, deceiving, and being deceived." (2 Timothy 3:13) (NLT)

So, at that point, he was doing nothing but "stealing" from me. I felt robbed of my first real love relationship, my virginity, my first church wedding, my time of being a wife first before being a mother, and my first real honeymoon. As I look back over just this part of my story, although he was my first in everything, it was as if anything involving him concerning me resulted in things being taken.

Instead of things being added to me while making me happy, he stole from me with false promises.

I did an internet study on the narcissist and found out it is called the "Black Spider Web." A narcissist is like a spider that creates a delicate spider web to trap a person. Once inside the spider's web, the narcissist demands total control, and they continuously test their victims to get them to show loyalty by allowing themselves to be controlled. Crazy as it sounds, in the beginning with a narcissist, you may see the mind games and control of "OTHER" people before you see yourself as being controlled. (Narcissistabusesupport. com).

I think about this above study and look back over my 35 years of marriage and how Deacon Todd treated me and how he made me feel. It was identical to the black spider web process. I was his victim who was trapped in his web by control and manipulation. Below were the steps:

- He preyed on me. He was interested only because of his lust, but he was not in love with me. He targeted me and all my innocence. His empty love was based on what I could bring to the table - good job, nice car, good credit, and monies all for his use.

- He built a web. The web was made up of all his smooth-talking, empty promises, deception, and lies he told me. Was it just his way to lure me towards the web to be captured?
- He pursued me with love bombing. This consisted of gift-giving, trips, nice dinners, acting as if he really loved and was concerned about me, and only wanted the best for me.
- He captures me. With deception, he impregnates me on purpose and causes me to become more entangled in his demonic web by pressuring me to be in covenant with him as his wife.
- The abuse. He used misuse, disrespect, rejection, abandonment, infidelity, treated me like his property, manipulated and controlled me as he tried to break and keep me down. He raped my soul and tried to suck all the God-life out of me while trying to set me up for the final kill that didn't work!
- Looked for another supply source from other victims. He used infidelity.

It may sound eerie and crazy, but it played out just like the black spider web process. I had become his next victim on the web through control and manipulation. His assignment was to kill me by sucking the life out of me after years of silent abuse and by killing anything and everything of God I carried while being entangled in his demonic web.

We started our first chapter of marriage off with a child on the way because of the full-blown deception towards me wrapped in disfunction and full of meaningless empty love. I got confirmation quickly down the road as we moved forward as husband and wife. Most of his words and promises were empty and rarely or never happened, as he said. If they did, it was off my dime and not his. Although when things were fruitful off my dime, he would surely and quickly take credit for it before people to try and compliment the false image of himself.

I began to question what was all of this? I came from a two-parent home, and what I was experiencing and dealing with in my covenant from Deacon Todd was strange for me. But it was my first marriage, so I had nothing to compare it with. So, I went through the motions, and that was all I knew how to do. Was all this execution just a sinister plot and a part of satan's plan to try and destroy me at the hands of my ex-lover, husband, and friend? The more I write and tell my story, it's as if the real story is unfolding.

It seems truly clear to me now. It seemed like a deliberate set-up to entangle, lock me in, and then kill me.

Let's go over his steps. We dated. Soon after, he came into the church with me, or now should I say, "for me." I started to feel controlled and smothered like his property and not his equal. I gave him some space. He got baptized, he proposed, I accepted, bad habits manifested again, I gave the ring back, he pursued harder, then sped things up in the relationship. He came home on a visit, impregnated me off full-blown deception, lied to my parents, and we got married. I wonder how he felt. Did he feel like he achieved much knowing he lied, trapped and tricked a young, pretty, innocent little church girl? What a confused and messed up individual he was.

To me, Deacon Todd had it down perfectly and knew precisely what his assignment was concerning me. He knew exactly what he was doing and how he was going to do it to try to destroy me and my purpose. He tried to take me further away from the center of God's will and plans for my life because of his brokenness and sicknesses. It's very apparent he was sent in my life to try to destroy me, and everything in me that resembled God. What a very cold-hearted, evil, sinister, and selfish individual!

From the outside looking in, our relationship appeared healthy and loving. But on the inside, it was a very selfish, cold-hearted, dark-plotted, abusive, demonic, demeaning, degrading, shameful, disrespectful, and hurtful relationship. It was all so deceptive and evil! It was if I was married to two different people. The first one was the fake Christian, well versed in the word of God and was the nicest person you ever wanted to meet. He did nice things for anyone while being the most comfortable person to talk to. The other person was an angry, hateful, selfish, hurting and broken individual.

Sporadically, Deacon Todd would share intimate secrets with me about his childhood. He told me about his grandfather's infidelity when he was married to his grandmother and his dad's infidelity and physical abuse towards his mom as a little boy. His real dad left him and his siblings when they were young. He had multiple stepsiblings because of his dad's infidelity, who also had another family across town.

The sad part was he wanted to talk about the issues, but he didn't want to get the help he needed to deal with it each day. He needed healing and deliverance. Despite all the brokenness and hurt, I saw in him from his past. He chose to cover up and maintain this false image of himself as being confident, secure, and a totally in control man. Unfortunately, he was the total opposite of all those things because the person he was trying so hard to be didn't even exist.

I heard his aunt speak well of Deacon Todd and his brothers. She commented they were not like their father. They were good boys. It would have made sense for Deacon Todd not to repeat what he had seen his grandfather and dad do to their wives, but it was generational and never dealt with or broken off him. Because it wasn't dealt with and left him scarred and hurt, he repeated exactly what he saw his grandfather and father do to their families. Why? Because broken and hurting people do break and hurt other people.

Although I thought he was my soulmate, destiny partner, and covering, in reality, he was the opposite. He was working against me with lies, betrayal, and jealousy. His assignment in my life was as a destiny stealer, killer and destroyer masked as a true believer in the church and around the community.

Sharon L. Johnson

Why Did He Marry Me?

We were husband and wife. At the time, I didn't understand how I had become entangled and entrapped in Deacon Todd's demonic web/trap. I didn't know how I got there and didn't realize the necessity and urgency to get out or how to get out. For me, it was only the beginning of a demonic journey with Deacon Todd.

What had I allowed to be attached to me for this committed life of marriage promised before God? Had I allowed an abandoned, rejected, wounded, broken, and hurting little boy with insecurities, fatherless, and no real identity to attach himself to me? Or had he deliberately been sent in my life on a sinister, demonic assignment from Lucifer to "stop, abort, steal, kill, and destroy" my destiny and anything God-like about me? It would all begin to unfold and make sense as our marriage progressed.

I began to live my life with Deacon Todd, the only way I knew how. When we started dating, I noticed how he pulled me away from my family and friends and continued to do so during our marriage. He kept reassuring me with words and actions that he would love me, provide, and care for me. According to him, I wouldn't need anything.

As he pulled me away from my village, he built his own. He wanted me to be around his family and in his circle. That circle consisted of his friends and their spouses. A few of them were on the outside, but most were in the church. To build himself a secure village, it seemed as if he always befriended weak, carnal, or "yes" people in the church, outside of the church, and in the community. People in his village saw his ungodly lifestyle but didn't make him accountable. They were the ones who had the same carnal lifestyle as he did. They were the ones who were so infatuated with the words he spoke and his teachings while they witnessed him not applying what he taught to his own life. They were the ones he used financially if he could. They were the ones who wanted to be just like him because of all the material things they thought he possessed. The level of respect for him and his false image was at a very crazy high standard as they saw him live a double life right in front of them and in the church. It was not normal. Actually, it was demonic to the point where it seemed as if they revered him like a god.

The word of God says in 1 Peter 1:16 (NKJV) that we are to "Be ye holy for I am holy." Where was the conviction on both ends? Also, in 2 Timothy 3:1-9 (NLT) it says, "They will act religious, but they will reject the power could make them godly. Stay away from people like that!" Apparently, the influence he had over them blinded their eyes to the double life he lived in front of them. They didn't know, so they patted him on the back for getting away with all the wicked, deceptive, and hurtful things he was doing to people within his family and within the church. Those were the types of people in his village.

I wasn't allowed to really go anywhere, but Deacon Todd was always in an out. I remember a time when my two sisters were going to New Mexico to see our brother. Deacon Todd gave me fits and didn't let me go. I was so hurt behind that because I didn't understand why he acted that way.

During our marriage, it was too much like right for Deacon Todd to respect me out of the gate as his wife in church. He began to lie and tell people in the church that he only married me because he got me pregnant! Of course, I heard some of the church members say it a few years into the marriage, but I had no idea it originated with Deacon Todd. Why did he marry me? What was his purpose because I sure didn't push or want it? My mother didn't even want Deacon Todd to marry me because of the pregnancy, but he insisted and begged while saying he wanted to make things right. Why? What was his real intent? As I write about it, I get chills because the whole thing seems so cold, plotted out, and sinister.

All his subtle kindness was just the beginning to set things in motion for his full-blown control and manipulation to easily be in play during the marriage. When I was in it, all the kindness and giving made me feel secure and confident that he really had me and was taking care of me. All I needed to do was to go to him, and no one else because I knew he had me. Manipulation! It was all a setup! Although he did very nice things for me indirectly, he made me feel as if I was his property. In my dysfunctional subconsciousness, it was a reassurance that this guy loved me, and I was the only one. (Toxic thinking.)

After our first child was born, things started off well like we were a family. But eventually, I was a single parent because he was always busy at the church, on a church auxiliary, and never at home or either out with the brothers—so he said.

Manipulation, control, and brainwashing were being used at its highest level. Deacon Todd was always nice and slow and subtle at how he went about doing things for me to get what he wanted from me. When he did things for me, he always expected or assumed something in return. He knew I was a giving person.

I thought we were a power team, and we were in this together to win it through the good and bad. In previous conversations, while dating, I remember Deacon Deacon Todd would always say, "Let's never bring up divorce because it won't happen to us." However, I found out from a few of the women he had been unfaithful with who said the words to them "divorcing me" was pretty much the first thing that came out of his mouth. It was one of his pickup lines for women to get their attention along with him not having on his wedding ring.

He knew when and how to say the right things when it came to our marriage, but because of all the deception, his actions and the words never lined up after we were in the covenant.

We would have consistent conversations, where we talked about things and areas in our covenant that we both could improve on to satisfy each other. I let Deacon Todd know what things would make me happier in our relationship. He would listen and say he would do better, but I never saw any manifestation. All I heard were empty promises that he would do better. After I heard from some of the women who he was unfaithful with, I discovered the things I told him would make me happy are things he did for those women.

It was so second nature for him to flatter and gracefully build other people up, especially the opposite sex who were right in the church. He was very disrespectful to me. I felt like Deacon Todd's property and not his wife. He was a charmer who felt very confident at it. He had wandering eyes and was very flirtatious with other women in and outside of the church.

Deacon Todd found it so easy to continuously break down his children and me when no one was around. He could only find fault in our children and told them what they weren't going to be and what they couldn't do. I remember many times when the children were in tears because of his words towards them. In Proverbs 18:21 (KJV), it says, "Death and life are in the power of the tongue." You would think because he knew scripture, it would be applied to his family, but he never did. He was particularly good at consciously breaking us down and found no difficulty in doing so. Although he enjoyed being built up by others, he didn't choose to do that for his family.

As I am writing, I understand that was another obvious way of him feeling empowered and in control of his family by speaking and tearing us down to make us feel inferior to him while keeping us underneath him. The word of God tells us in Colossians 3:21 (PHILLIPS), "Fathers, don't over-correct your children, or they will grow up feeling inferior and frustrated." He also had the title of a Deacon, although he wasn't living the life of a Deacon. "He must manage his own family well and see his children obey him, and he must do so in a manner worthy of full respect. If anyone does not know how to manage his own family, how can he take care of God's church?" (1 Timothy 3:4-5) (NIV). He wasn't there for me; he wasn't protecting and covering me. He wasn't providing for me as a god-fearing husband should have been. Why was he doing things to his family on the inside of his home contrary to what the word of God had instructed him to do, but on the outside, he acted as if he lived by and applied the word of God when it concerned his wife and his family. In reality, that was not the case at all. "Do not merely listen to the word, and so deceive yourselves. Do what it says." (James 1:22) (NIV)

Everything about Deacon Todd's life was an oxymoron. There was a good side and an evil side to him.

"A double-minded man is unstable in all his ways." (James 1:8). Think about this. How do you think any union would be if you were in covenant with your head, your provider, your covering, your protector, your lover, and friend who lived two lives and was double-minded? Behind closed doors, the constant manipulation and control coming from the evil Deacon Todd felt like a continual stripping and tearing down for his family and me. But I'm sure in his mind, he was feeling in control and empowered almost like a god because his family was right where he wanted them to be. They were fearful, miserable, and underneath him. "He will oppose and exalt himself over everything that is called God or is worshiped, so (that) he sets himself up in God's temple, proclaiming himself to be God." (2 Thessalonians 2:4) (NIV)

The sad part was, this spiritual husband and father didn't see how satan used him to destroy his entire family unit? When it came to their identity in Christ, their purpose and the calls God had upon their lives? "Lo, children are a heritage of the Lord, and the fruit of the womb is his reward." (Psalms 127:3). "The children of thy servants shall continue, and their seed shall be established before thee. (Psalms 102:28). As God-fearing parents, we are on assignment in our children's lives to cover, nurture, and protect them and the gifts they carry inside. Our assignment is not to tear them down by speaking death over them.

Satan is so cunning and presents things as if they were good, but they go against man, against humanity, and against God. There was a lot of manipulation, control, and dysfunction going on. Because the kids were so young, they didn't see it. By the time they were older, they had lived in this disfunction for so long, they probably thought it was okay. There would be a season of tear and breakdown, and then there would be a season of moving on and acting as if nothing was ever done or said while doing kind things for us. Sadly, in most cases, there was never a season of building back up that which had been torn down. There were times when I wanted to spend some travel time with my sisters or family, and he didn't want me to go. He acted as if he wanted me to just spend time with him. But mind you, we would always travel with his family, which was just another manipulative control move. We would have wonderful road trips and vacations as a family for the children in the beginning, which appeared to the outside that we had the perfect family unit. But there was a lot of dysfunction going on behind the scenes in our home that no one saw. Although Deacon Todd taught the Bible and knew how to apply it to everyone else's life situation, it wasn't being taught, walked out, or applied in our own home by him. The word says, "A fool does not care whether he understands a thing or not. All he wants to do is show how smart he is..." (Proverbs 18:2) (GNT)

I never knew which person I would be dealing with from day to day. Imagine the anxiety, the feeling of walking on eggshells as Deacon Todd's wife to make sure I did everything right, so there was no confrontation, rage, and anger so the evil side wouldn't manifest. Because of the spirits I was dealing with and Deacon Todd not being the real person he was pretending to be, I didn't really have a fair chance out of the gate because of all the deception. It was all a part of his manipulation and control plan. I always felt I was in a "no-win" situation. I tried to do everything right. But instead of a compliment, I was met with an argument, finding fault, blame, an explosion of anger, commands to "shut up," correction in public, and condescending talk because I didn't do something the way he would have done it. Constant draining came with all the never-ending confrontation, manipulation, and control. It was though the spirits driving Deacon Todd made him gloat and smile because of the power he had over his family and me. I think he felt very empowered by intentionally doing all these abusive things to us. Yes, the same person stood with me before God and family and made promises to love, cherish, obey, and take care of me for the rest of his life.

I had given most of myself to this "great pretender and master manipulator." I didn't even realize early on that I had lost myself in the marriage. Because he was so in love with himself and his false image, he wasn't ever in love with me. How could he be? It was really just a lust thing, and he just wanted to use, abuse and keep me underneath him spiritually, naturally, and financially because that made him look good and feel like a big man.

Go Through Season

All this silent abuse from my covenant partner caused me to run into the arms of God and establish an intimate relationship with Him, so I could grow. Although the enemy may have sent it to try and destroy or stop me, God used it all for His good to birth the worshipper, prophetic, intercession, fasting, and a strong prayer life in me. God knew what I needed, and when I needed it. He is always on time. That's what I love about Him. God always has a plan. He is always working it out for our good, even when it doesn't seem or feel like it. He is God and His thoughts are not our thoughts, neither are our ways His ways. The Lord says. "For as the heavens are higher than the earth, so are my ways higher than your ways and my thoughts than your thoughts." (Isaiah 55:9) (KJV)

That is how my story went and how it was supposed to end, but God! "You intended to harm me, but God intended it for good." (Genesis 50:20) (NIV). It may have caused me to be shattered and broken, but God is using my pain, brokenness, and desperation for His purpose and His glory.

Wow, as I write this story, I didn't realize until now that when we dated Deacon Todd he said he wanted to find a good church girl to marry, I would be that girl. Those words sounded like an indirect compliment, but what was entailed and came with so much disrespect, hurt, and abuse that it made me feel like his victim rather than his love mate.

Pursued In Love Or Lust?

When I met Deacon Todd, he seemed like a very regular guy and we just clicked. It might have been love at first sight if that really does exist. He seemed to have a lot of potential, came very well packaged, spoke well, and was easy to talk to. When he conversed with me, it was if his words drew me in. He knew how to do all the right things to make my heart flutter with butterflies whenever we talked or saw each other. I couldn't get enough of him; he was always on my mind with thoughts of when we would be together again. I didn't realize or even understand, at that time, I was selected to be his next lust and sex victim, not his love partner at all. All the while, he kept reassuring me of his love and all the big plans he had for both of us.

Just in case you are questioning what the difference is between "lust" and "love," **Lust** is having an "intense sexual desire" or "appetite" for someone. **Love** is an intense "feeling" of deep affection for someone "attraction" that includes sexual desire. This love is unconditional affection with no limits or conditions. Because the definitions are remarkably close, you could easily be confused.

Remember the story of Tamar, King David's

daughter, and her brother Amnon raped her? He had become obsessed with her beauty and only wanted her sexually. After he laid with her, he hated her even the more than he loved her. That was surely lust. Saying you love a person and being in love with an individual, is entirely two different things. DISCERN and know when someone is pursuing you in lust or is genuinely pursuing you because they love you. Now as I look back at my covenant, he surely wasn't in love with me, he only lusted after me and was in love with what I could bring and add to him and his fake image of himself and all of his full-blown deception and acting that he was walking in. Innocently and unknowingly, I had allowed myself to become entrapped into an abusive relationship at the hands of a Christian narcissist. Because I thought it was love and it felt like love in the beginning, but it was far from it. It felt as if I had allowed and given my heart to a Judas, and he knew what his assignment was regarding me and my destiny. It was if he was on a demonic and abortive assignment and had planned the entire 35 years of our marriage for my demise, and he was fully aware of it.

I Was In A Competition

When I went into covenant and said, "I do" to Deacon Todd, I didn't realize I included other spirits that came with the lust spirit already on him. It was accompanied by the spirit of infidelity from generational curses inherited from his father/grandfather. It also came with a pornography spirit, which is an adulterous spirit that comes with fantasy and is like a bottomless pit that can never be filled. In addition to those spirts, there was his own self-love and selfishness.

Entering into the covenant automatically placed me in the competition ring with all of the spirits I just mentioned, while making both of us feel, right out of the gate, as if I wasn't good enough for him. I was continually trying to satisfy Deacon Todd, but always felt I was falling short because of what I was in competition with.

Silent Abuse

My silent abuse happened while no one was around to see it. There was a lot of manipulation and control going on in our union behind closed doors. Deacon Todd had a real problem with anger and his temper. When we would have an argument, he would throw fits of anger, and his level of rage included throwing and punching, which resulted in things being broken up in our home. I was fearful of him early on in our covenant. As I look back, it was just a form of manipulation he was using on me. Of course, I never saw that side of him while we were dating. He began to use negative words to subtly put me down as he corrected me. He tried to tear me and my self-esteem down bit by bit mentally, emotionally, naturally, and spiritually so. Earlier I mentioned everything about a Christian narcissist is an oxymoron, while he was trying to keep me down with his negative words, he thrived from people's positive comments about him to stay built up.

His silent abuse towards me seemed intentional, sinister, cold-blooded, and so second nature for him. While he wore a church title, he worked hard and diligently in church leadership and along with the Pastor. It was as if he had lost or no longer was afraid for God. "There is no fear of God before their eyes." (Romans 3:18) (ESV). He had so many other people fooled. It was as if he felt God could not see what he was doing. It was all so unhealthy, toxic, and demonically scary for me. It was time for me to exit the union. It was so bad, I felt as though life was being sucked out of me because of the manipulation and levels of warfare that I was up against. All of this came from my husband, who laid next to me in the bed and kept reassuring me of his love for me. "For our struggle is not against enemies of blood and flesh, but against the rulers, against the authorities, against the cosmic powers of this present darkness, against the spiritual forces of evil in the heavenly places (Ephesians 6:12) (ESV).

    It got so bad I felt I was married to Lucifer himself. The Lord wanted me to do a study on Lucifer and his fall. Many parts of that story, and the characteristics of Lucifer, reminded me of how much of it I was in covenant with, and how my husband thought, how he operated, and how he acted. It was mind-blowing to see him behave like Lucifer while masked up and going through the motions of being a Christian. When I studied about Lucifer, I noticed a narcissist has similar characteristics like Lucifer had, which will be discussed in a later chapter.

Unequally Yoked

I was in a toxic, dysfunctional marriage covenant with an individual who wanted to keep me down and underneath him spiritually because of his own weaknesses, insecurities, past hurts, abandonment, and rejection issues. However, we serve a faithful God and He allowed my covenant to come crashing down to a much-needed end. I didn't see the end of it as a good thing in the beginning. It shook my very core and turned my world upside down for the bad, so I thought. Some months after the divorce, I understood it was all for my good!

Who Was I In Covenant With?

Who, or what, should I say I got into covenant with? I thought Deacon Todd was a perfect gentleman who spoke well and was easy to talk to. He knew how and what to say to influence people and get what he wanted as well as portray himself in a positive light throughout the community, family, and church. Deacon Todd seemed very experienced with life. On the outside, he appeared to be the nicest guy around; however, there was a "public" face and a "private" face (which I will discuss in a later chapter). This is the man I had given my heart to, and he was a fake and a pretender.

The level of deception he walked in was full-blown and sinister. He was a person of multiple personalities living a life of lies under a fake identity he created for himself that didn't even exist. He found it so easy to thrive off someone else's identity and whatever other benefits came with it. Deacon Todd covered himself, or should I say he hid, under the umbrella of a religious church where people could not see that he wore the mask of a God-fearing Christian in a Godly covenant, but he cheated on me, lied to me, deceived me, used and abused me. He counseled and advised others with Godly counsel. Also, he preached, taught, and debated the Word of God with anyone who wanted to challenge or listen to him. He was always ready as 1 Peter 3:15 says, "To give an answer to every man who asketh you a reason of the hope that is in you with meekness and fear..."

I know that's confusing, right? Why would you and how do you serve two masters when the Word of God clearly says in Matthew 6:24, "No man can serve two masters: for either he will hate the one, and love the other or else he will hold to one, and despise the other. Ye cannot serve God and mammon."

It was as if everything he did was like an oxymoron. He lived a Christian life in front of people, but when no one was around, he lived a secret life. He wore the mask of a Christian but underneath the cover was nothing but darkness (very selfish and self-absorbed). He knew the Word of God but didn't apply it to his own life. He could give you Godly teaching and counsel on your finances, relationships, etc. and tell you how to change your situation, but he could/would never apply his own counsel and advice to his life and position to bring about positive change. "If you are looking for advice, stay away from fools..." (Proverbs 14:7) (TLB)

1 King 18:21 (BSB) "Then Elijah approached all the people and said, "How long will you waver between two opinions? If the LORD is God, follow Him. But if Baal is God, follow him. But the people did not answer a word."

Since we have been given confirmation in the Word of God about the importance of a made-up mind as to who you are going to serve, why would a person who teaches and expounds on the Word not want their walk and talk to line up? Why would you want to portray yourself as a Christian, but live a lifestyle of a sinner? Or preach, teach, and reach everyone outwardly but have a closet life. "But be doers of the word, and not a doer, he is like a man who looks intently at his natural face in a mirror. For he looks at himself and goes away and at once forgets what he was like." (James 1:22-24) (ESV)

It was too much. He became like Dr. Jekyll and Mr. Hyde. I didn't know who he was anymore. In front of people, he was so humble, kind, God-fearing and would do anything for anybody. Deacon Todd was an all-around nice guy, but at home he had a temper, and most of the time his words tore and broke down our family. "Life and death are in the power of the tongue." (Proverbs 18:21) (NIV) He seemed more concerned about his false image in front of men and what they thought about him than what God saw about his real image. He worked extremely hard at maintaining a nice guy image in front of people.

Paul asked a question in Galatians 1:10 (KJV), and he also answered this question very nicely to address a person's double identity while serving in ministry. "For do I now persuade men or God? or do I seek to please men? for if I yet pleased men, I should not be the servant of Christ." Over Deacon Todd's life, I believe it became natural and comfortable for him to live a life full of secrets because he had done it for so long. Although people saw the ungodly things Deacon Todd did in deception towards others and his family, no one ever called him out or made him accountable.

He was forever studying and learning, but it was if he could never come to the knowledge of the truth. (2 Timothy 3:7). He could recall the Word by memory, but the Word wasn't in him. He wasn't making conscious choices to apply the Word of God to his own life. "Anyone who listens to the Word but does not do what it says is like someone who looks at his face in a mirror and, after looking at himself, goes away and immediately forgets what he looks like." (James 1:24) (NIV)

Please Hear My Cry

It gives me chills as I am writing this part, to clearly see that all this was a part of satan's sinister plan for my life. A plan to trap me into covenant with the wrong one then use that covenant partner to purposely try and stop me from walking into my full identity and call. Time was of absolutely no importance to him at all. His assignment was just to get it done. (Wow!)

There were many things that I really enjoyed doing, which seemed to give Deacon Todd great pleasure and joy to try and stop me and from being who I was. It was as if he was trying to hold me back while trying to conform me into who he wanted me to be and to do things his way. He was very jealous of me and would subtly throw me under the bus when he could. He always wanted to take credit for anything we did together. I always noticed he never gave God glory or praise for much of anything.

It was so evident that he didn't want me to thrive and be what God had called me to be because he feared it would make him look bad and he wanted to keep me beneath him. He was really concerned about his image in people's eyes more than he was concerned about his image in God's eyes. There was so much down-low intimidation, jealousy, and competition in our union coming from him towards me, and his own words confirmed it. It didn't matter to him how he did it eventually, just if it worked. If it meant isolating me from family and friends, betraying me, shaming me, disrespecting me, deceiving me, lying to me, abandoning me, rejecting me, degrading me, abusing and making me feel unloved/unwanted. He didn't care just as long as it consumed me and my life or distracted me and as long as it stopped me from walking in purpose.

Master Manipulator

It was so toxic and demonic how he could turn these personalities on and off along with his emotions, just like water. I was in a covenant with a master manipulator, who was very skilled at it and did it exceptionally well in his home when no one was around. But God did say in the last days, "For false Christ's and false prophets will arise and perform great signs and wonders, to lead astray, if possible, even God's chosen ones." (Matthew 24:24) That is what I dealt with throughout pretty much of the marriage. Each day I didn't know who he was going to pretend to be. Was he going to be kind and love on me today and play out the Christian character? Or was he going to be mean and hateful, confrontational, finding fault, and blame me for everything as he played out the role of satan? All of that back and forth was very draining and made me feel as if I was walking on eggshells to keep things peaceful with him and within the house. It was very draining, emotionally and mentally.

Deacon Todd would become angry quickly, which was a form of manipulation to instill fear in me. Once when our children were small, he threatened my life if I ever left him, as he held a knife to me while one of our daughters watched. Why didn't I run or tell someone? I was afraid, and I wasn't going to leave my girls behind. If I said I was leaving, he would reply, "You can leave, but you're not taking the girls!"

After a while, it was if God was opening my spiritual eyes to giving me more revelation and understanding about the spirit realm. When I looked at my situation in the natural realm, it made no sense at all. Who wants to be well versed in the Word and not use it in your everyday life? Unless that person is well versed in the Word for other personal reasons that would benefit them in getting what they wanted from others. Ponder on that.

Financial Woes

When Deacon Todd and I were dating, it was if the monies were plenty. When we went into covenant, that is when our finances began to struggle. I had come into the covenant with a very good paying job and he had just gotten out of the Marine Corps and his track record on jobs; were very inconsistent and adding very little to our finances. We discussed our bills and decided how to make sure they would get paid on time. He would talk with our Pastor quite a bit by himself for counsel. I just looked at it as him getting good counsel to make sure he was doing this new husband thing correct. As we discussed our finances further, he tells me that our Pastor had instructed us to keep our bills separate. What new married couple starts off being divided; especially in their finances? I do not believe that our Pastor had given him those instructions. Plus, it totally goes against the word of God and what he says about couples becoming one in unity. "With all humility and gentleness, with patience, bearing with one another in love, eager to maintain the "unity" of the Spirit in the bond of peace." (Ephesians 4:2-3) (ESV) "And over all these virtues put on love, which binds them all together in perfect unity."

Colossians 3:14 (ESV) Unity is a closeness between two fully integrated people who are separate; yet engaged in a shared enterprise. Although Deacon Todd had gotten married; his mindset and thinking was still single; especially when it came to his finances. Plus, if our finances were kept separate, it would have helped him to have his own extra money needed to continue his lifestyle of singleness, even though he was married to me.

Christian Narcissist?

While surfing the internet, God allowed me to stumble across an article on YouTube entitled, "What is a Narcissist (Black Spider)?" I began to listen to it, and my mouth dropped. Everything they were saying, even down to the illustrations, told my story and what I had just come out of. I was in awe, but I heard the spirit of the Lord say, "This is what you were in covenant with, and it is why I released you out of it." I was in covenant with a Narcissist!?!? (Read 2 Timothy 3:2-8 Jude 1:4 Proverbs 2:12-15) I said, "Lord, but I don't even know what a narcissist is." I began to do an extensive study and later found out there are several different narcissists, and a Christian narcissist was one of them. A Christian narcissist is a non-believer who wears a mask of a Christian who is well versed in the Word but does not live by it. The person is self-absorbed, selfish, prideful and puts God second as they believe they are their own god.

I was so outdone and began to go into praise because God removed me from a life and death situation. When He did it, I was unscathed and didn't look like what I had been through. As I continued researching this topic, many of my unanswered questions were answered, and many missing links that didn't make sense in the marriage started to connect and make sense. I got clarity and a much better understanding enabling me to get closure about what all I had just come out of. Not only that, but it confirmed to me that being released from the covenant was undoubtedly a strategic move of God, I needed to save my life!

God then had me look at the story of satan and parallel the study to a Christian narcissist. Oh wow! I realized satan and a Christian narcissist were like identical twins and had the same characteristics.

Let me give you a little history of both.

<u>Narcissism</u> is the pursuit of gratification from vanity or egotistic admiration of one's idealized self-image and attributes. This includes self-flattery, perfectionism, "PRIDE," and arrogance. The term originated from Greek mythology, where the young Narcissus fell in love with his own image reflected in a pool of water. Although the devil is present in some form in many religions and can be compared to some mythological gods, he's best known for his role in Christianity. In modern Biblical translations, the devil is the adversary of God and God's people.

Please Hear My Cry

<u>Lucifer</u> was once the closest to God in heaven. The word Lucifer comes from a Hebrew term that translates to "shining one." "He reflected the glory of God, just as the moon reflects the light of the sun. He was the seal of perfection, full of wisdom and perfect in beauty. He was perfect, resplendent, beautiful, and most important for the human understanding of him, he was, and is, an angel with all the accompanying attributes. (Ezekiel 28:12-19) (KJV)

But if God is perfect love, why would a being that's seen God's glory in person turn against him? Lucifer's heart became proud on account of his beauty, and he corrupted his wisdom because of his splendor. He became so impressed with his own beauty, intelligence, power, and position that he began to desire for himself the honor and glory that belonged to God alone. This most beautiful of all God's creations tried to take the throne in heaven and tried to rule creation in God's stead. It was self-generated "PRIDE" that struck him down. This pride represents the actual beginning of sin in the universe—preceding the fall of the human Adam by an indeterminate time. "Behold, as for the proud one, his soul is not right within him, but the righteous will live by his faith. Furthermore, wine betrays the haughty man, so he does not stay at home. He enlarges his appetite like Sheol, and he is like death, never satisfied. He also gathers to himself all nations and collects to himself all peoples." (Habakkuk 2:4-5) (NASB)

In Isaiah 14:12, it tells us Lucifer's choice before his fall. "I" will ascend to heaven. "I" will raise my throne above the stars of God "I" will sit on the mount of assembly on the heights of Zaphon I will ascend to the tops of the clouds, "I" will make myself like the Most High. Did you notice all of the "I wills" in this passage? He said he would exalt his throne above the stars of God. The word "stars" here does not refer to what we see in the night sky. It refers to the angels of God. In other words, "I will take over heaven, I will be God." That is Lucifer/Satan's sin and is the iniquity found in him. He does not want to be God's servant. He does not want to do what he was created to do. He wants to be served, and millions have chosen to do just that, serve him. Some people have listened to his lies and decided to follow him.

Just from that little bit of research, it is clear that a Christian narcissist and Lucifer are definitely one of the same persons. These two individuals have so much in common, even upon my research, it was made very clear that this was all so toxic and demonic and had satan's handprints all on it. Lucifer was very prideful and surely caught up in his looks and intelligence, which he used to lure people into serving him. One-third of the angels were removed with him from heaven. Because of this heinous sin against God, satan's power became completely perverted. (Isaiah 14:12).

In Ezekiel 28, it says, "Thus says the Lord GOD: You were the signet of perfection, full of wisdom and perfect in beauty. You were in Eden, the garden of God. Every precious stone was your covering, carnelian, chrysolite, and moonstone, beryl, onyx, and jasper, sapphire, turquoise, and emerald and worked in gold were your settings and your engravings. On the day you were created, they were prepared. With an anointed cherub as guardian, I placed you were on the holy mountain of God. You walked among the stones of fire. You were blameless in your ways from the day you were created, until iniquity was found in you. "By the abundance of your traffic they filled the midst of you with violence, and you have sinned: therefore, I have cast you as profane out of the mountain of God; and I have destroyed you, O covering cherub, from the midst of the stones of fire." Ezekiel 28:16 (ESV)

The above very much applies to a Christian narcissist also. Satan's goal in both cases is to gather to himself all nations and collect to himself all people – to himself and away from God – even though Satan knows full well those people will be utterly destroyed as a result. (Habakkuk 2:5) Below is a list of similar characteristics of Lucifer and a Christian narcissist:

- They have insolent pride, which is where there is no limit to their desire for being exalted by others. They are the ultimate "kingdom builders," intending to show their "greatness." The only thing limiting them is their opportunity. This is why classic narcissists like Hitler and Napoleon could be obscure. But when given a chance, they would move quickly to create the biggest kingdom possible and at the expense of many other people, of course.

- Narcissists are charmers and excellent conversationalists with the ones they take an interest in as their next victim. Their words are smooth as butter as they are trying to build their confidence up in you while making you feel as if they are only concerned about your needs. On the outside, they are neat and well-dressed. This is how people perceive them and it's especially important. They love attention, they love to be out front, they love to brag about themselves, and they love compliments. They are very prideful, master manipulators, abusers, controllers, and liars. Narcissists are love bombers at the beginning of a relationship. Love bombing is an attempt to influence a person by demonstrations of lots of attention and affection. "But evil men and seducers shall wax worse and worse, deceiving, and being deceived." (2 Timothy 3:13)

- In my studies about Lucifer, I found "Lucifer could charm the birds from the trees and then chew them up and spit out the feathers." In a nightclub, he could be surrounded by beautiful women, who he approached with charm, then speak praises to each that would melt every woman's heart. He can serenade and seduce with a classic line, "Tell me what you most desire? " Lucifer's philosophy of "love them and leave them" means only those useful to him get to keep his attention.

- Lucifer became so impressed with his own beauty, intelligence, power, and the position he began to desire for himself the honor and glory belonged to God alone. The sin corrupted Lucifer was self-generated pride.

In Ezekiel 28:12, 15, 17), it tells us this king was a created being and left the creative hand of God in a perfect state, and he remained perfect in his ways until iniquity was found in him (verse 15b). "Your heart became proud on account of your beauty, and you corrupted your wisdom because of your splendor."

- The sweeping gesture: Narcissist/Lucifer loves to impress mere mortals by doing nice things for them but it is just as important for them to remind you, so you won't forget what they did and how they helped you.

- They won't admit when they are wrong, and they're always blaming someone else because each time, it's someone else's fault. In the eyes of Lucifer/Christian narcissist, everyone is not as intelligent as they are. While there may be a few exceptions, Lucifer/Christian narcissist lacks any inner ability to reflect on his actions. His forte is failing to follow procedure and then justifying his behavior and the irrelevance of the rules of engagement.

- Envy of other relationships. Lucifer/Narcissist spends a lot of energy denigrating and criticizing people. They primarily target people who have a real relationship and have been sent to make him accountable and return him to Hell so the order is restored in the universe.
- Everything, including the empathy, is about a payoff for them: With only one exception in the first series (no spoilers), all Lucifer's/Christian narcissist actions are about the payoff. At first, they are trying to seduce, but later they are trying to understand what their victim has that makes them so special and immune to their charms.
- Their conversation is all about them. At every turn, Lucifer/Christian narcissist turns each conversation into their favorite topic, themselves.
- They are incredibly good looking. Lucifer is tall, dark, and handsome. He wears suits, the cut of which would make James Bond feel scruffy and underdressed. While his black corvette isn't an Aston Martin, it suits the slick image. Even without his supernatural charms, very few women would be

able to resist an advance.

- The needs of other people don't matter: To Lucifer, the world is quite literally his oyster. He has obviously made a lot of money. He can have anything or anyone he wants. All his relationships, including Dekker's young daughter, are based on his needs. As the disgraced son of God and ruler of Hell, he has a superiority complex and self-importance which no one on Earth can match.

Just to expound a little more about narcissistic abuse and how they will treat you, below are a few of the ways they manipulate and control. At the beginning of the relationship, with a Christian narcissist, it seems so right. They make you feel as if this is what true love is all about. The gifts, dinners, trips, over excessive compliments, and whatever else they deem necessary are designed to catch you, and that is what they will do. This is love-bombing. When your heart has been captured, the relationship will seem good for a while, until they are sure they have all your heart, confidence, and mind. Then the narcissist will slowly begin to manifest into who they really are. Because they have your heart, and your vision is blinded, it's tough to see the real person evolving through the manifestation.

- They will no longer be selfless individuals but become very selfish individuals they have always been who are only concerned about taking care of themselves and not you. (Example - Household only has one car and you let them use it with an understanding that they drop you off at work and pick you up. He does as requested and when it is time to pick you up from work, the person is one hour late with all kinds of excuses for being late.)

- They will refuse to take responsibility because it is never their fault. They will blame you for everything. (Example - They may say or do some hurtful things to you. If your feelings are hurt, it's not their fault, it's your fault, for having feelings)

- They are habitual liars. (Examples - They lie to make themselves look good, they lie to get out of responsibility, lie to manipulate and gain influence, they just lie out of habit.)

- They are prideful, condescending, elitist, and superior as they look down on you to make themselves feel more significant. They hide their disdain to prevent a loss of popularity. (Example - Narcissist in the working class look down on those with more money, educated narcissist, dismiss the opinions of those who have no degree.) Whatever a narcissist has (or think they have) is used to look down on others.)

- They're two-faced having a real face (private) and a stage (public) face. Neither is anything like the other. (Example - They can be charming, and they know how to gain favor with their stage face. Anyone who doesn't know them well will tell you they are the nicest, intelligent, and greatest person they have ever met. Anyone who knows them better, especially the one(s) under their abuse, will tell you how frustrating, toxic, evil, and sinister they are.

Note: Being the only one experiencing a narcissist's real face, while all other family members, friends, or co-workers can still only see the narcissist's stage face is a lonely, painful and frustrating place to be.

- They are very vindictive. Narcissists do not like to be questioned or asked to provide things like healthy boundaries and honesty. If they feel offended or crossed, it angers them, and you become an enemy. Yes, then the "Mr. or Ms. Wonderful" mask immediately comes off and they will stoop to any level to punish you.

- Narcissists project psychologically. They are full of accusations and criticisms. The most crazy-making thing about a narcissist's claim is that their complaint is precisely what they are doing. (Example - Have they just lied to you? Well, you are about to be called dishonest. Have they cheated you out of an opportunity? Well, you're going to get the finger pointed at you for being sneaky. And don't dare say a word to them about something hurtful they have done to you, because that makes you an abuser.)

They will make you feel as if you are walking on eggshells in your home because you can't do anything right in their eyes. Regardless of how hard you try, you are still in a no-win situation with them. They will try to make you seem like you are crazy. It's manipulation and one of the many ways they try to keep you beneath them. They continually strive to break you by tearing down your self-esteem with their conversation in low-key, subtle ways around other people. You will be the one constantly criticized severely and then called over sensitive if you show any feelings about it. Whatever they say or recommend, it's the law, and you don't know what you're talking about. If you disagree, that will be the start of an argument. This is just another form of manipulation to keep you beneath them. They make you feel as if they know/ have an answer for everything. Your opinion doesn't matter.

They smear people who oppose them. They are allergic to healthy boundaries and fairness. As mentioned above, if you question the insensitive things they do or put any limits whatsoever on their bad behavior, you will become an enemy, and they will target your social, professional, or personal obliteration. Whatever area in your life the narcissist perceives to be your weak spots, will be their prime targets. (Example - If the narcissist knows your greatest fear is social ridicule, that will be the main focus of the smear campaign. Or you made a mistake for which you feel guilty, that will be used against you.) The more effectively they can pinpoint your insecurities or flaws, the more successful they will be in eroding your confidence and your influence. It is always a power struggle for them.

Public Face/Private Face

A Christian narcissist masked non-believer has a Jekyll and Hyde personality. They have a nice side with kind words and selfless works on the outside in front of people. They also have an evil side that comes with manipulation, control, selfishness, anger, and rage on the inside. Only their victims experience this when no one is around. In public and around prominent people, they are privileged to see and experience the nice, selfless, kind side of them. In private and at home, the victim suffers the evil, hateful, selfish side of them. That's the way it's always played out.

If you have never been in a relationship with a narcissist and you hear a person talk about their abuse, it will sound off and crazy to you, especially if they know the person you are referring to. Most people have and will only see the public face (nice person). They haven't seen the private face you see and deal with daily so it makes you seem a little off, bitter, angry, hateful, unforgiving, and you're just trying to say hurtful things about the narcissist to make them look bad. But you are just trying to pour your heart out with all of the real truth about them.

What an eye-opener and sadness to know I had given all of myself to a Christian narcissist who wasn't concerned about me or even loved me for real. What really shook me was that he was so selfish and sinister and took a lot of pride and joy in wasting my precious time as he tried to hold me with no remorse.

You know how I mentioned earlier in the book, how he made me feel as if I was his property when we were dating. Well, in my studies of a Christian narcissist, that is precisely what they do. They search out someone who they feel can make their false image look good while making their love partner their victim and property. They will take that person's emotions and deliberately abused them without their consent; it is called emotional rape.

They will also try and use that person spiritually to steal their DNA, which includes your identity, your purpose, your destiny and your self-esteem and self-worth. Their demonic assignment in a person's life is to try and drain all of God out and kill you emotionally, mentally, financially, and spiritually.

I found it interesting that the goal of a Christian narcissist is to consume his victim. Because a narcissist cannot experience love on their own, they must harvest it from others. The way they do this is to disconnect their victims from all loved ones while sowing mistrust. Then they keep the victim in a perpetual state of self-doubt and confusion. This is done purposely to keep their victims tied to them and serving their needs continuously.

Christian narcissists are false prophets who come well versed in the Word of God wears the mask of a Christian, but underneath the cover, there is nothing about them that resembles God at all; there's only darkness. They are emotional and mental abusers who are very controlling and manipulative. They go through life lying and pretending to be someone or something they really are not. They work extremely hard at maintaining a false image of themselves over their brokenness for people. They are overly concerned with what people think about them and how people see them over what God sees and what he thinks about them. They are habitual liars who lie so bad they begin to believe their own lies. They are very good at hustling and getting over on good people to get what they want. They are "very" prideful, "very" selfish, and "very" self-absorbed people who don't like to submit to authority. Looking through the eyes of a narcissist, it is all about them and how the world revolves around them. They really think they are the most intelligent and that everyone else is beneath them. They walk around with a sense of entitlement and feel like people should bow down to them while making sure that all their needs are met. They feel as if you should be honored to serve them in whatever capacity. They think and act as if they are indispensable, and nothing or none can hurt them. They put themselves up there with God.

"Beloved, do not believe every spirit, but test the spirits to see whether they are from God, for many false prophets have gone out into the world." (1 John 4:1) (ESV)

Now imagine that person I just described wearing a mask of a Christian, very well versed in the Word of God, along with having a leadership title in the church. Just think about that. Very demonic, toxic, and explosive! What a dangerous, toxic combination the enemy has put together as dynamite to explode and kill, right in our churches. The results are broken covenants and families (and God hates divorces), many causalities (spiritual deaths where people aren't walking out their dreams or their calls because they are being held back), no identity (don't know who they are in Christ because of all the tearing down of their self-esteem's and character) and wasted time (biggest thing the enemy uses against us because you cannot get time back).

Sadly and truthfully, these Christian narcissists have been sent and are directly being used by satan to annihilate as many Christians as possible right in the church or their very own churches through self-sabotaging of their own ministries. They destroy their covenants and families with infidelity while leading people astray with double lifestyles, and intentionally connecting and marrying people with an abusive intent. Because of their brokenness, they can destroy people's lives, time, and purpose.

First Peter 5:8 tells us to be self-controlled and alert because our enemy prowls around like a roaring lion looking for someone to devour." He's not looking for the unbelievers because he already has them. He's looking for the believers. Do you see what satan's plan is and what he is doing right in the church? It is called spiritual espionage. "The wicked spies upon the righteous and seeks to kill him" (Psalm 37:32). (NASB) Satan has sent an army (Christian narcissist), who looks like us, who talks like us, has church titles, well versed in the Word, with abortive assignments to kill, steal and destroy the church right in the church.

Just a little more teaching about Christian narcissist and how dangerous, evil, and toxic they are. The title itself is an oxymoron, demonic and toxic. What do I mean? How can a person be a Christian (self-less like Christ) and a narcissist (selfish like Lucifer) at the same time? How do you wear two masks, a public one and a private one, at the same time? The most important question is, how do you serve two masters at the same time? When it says in Matthew 6:24, "No man can serve two masters for either he will hate the one and love the other or else he will hold to the one and despise the other. Ye cannot serve God and mammon."

A Christian narcissist has an evil heart, and not just an ordinary sinful heart of a person who messes up. What is an evil heart? It is a heart where someone deceives us with no conscious, hurts others with no remorse, spinning outrageous fabrications to ruin someone's reputation, or pretending they are spiritually committed yet has no fear of God before their eyes. They are experts at creating confusion and contention. They twist the facts, mislead, lie, avoid taking responsibility, deny reality, devise stories, and withhold information. (Psalms 5:8 Proverbs 6:13). They are experts at fooling others with their smooth speech and flattering words. (Psalms 50:19, Proverbs 12:5). They crave demand and control. Their highest authority is their own self-reverence. They use scripture to their own advantage, but they ignore and reject passages that might require self-correction and repentance. (Romans 2:8, Psalms 10). They play on the sympathies of good-willed people, often trumping the grace card. They have no empathy for the pain they have caused and no real intention of making amends or working hard to rebuild broken trust. (Proverbs 21:10, 1 Peter 2:16). They have no conscience and no remorse. They do not struggle against sin or evil; they delight in it. (Proverbs 2:14, Isaiah 32:6). He knows more true doctrine than you or I will ever know, but their heart is wicked because they do not believe it or live it. (2 Corinthians 11:13-15, Luke 3:8)

Just try and process that. How confusing, demonic, and toxic that really is, especially if you are in a relationship or marriage with a person who is pretending to be someone they are not. Confusion! They do not want to be exposed for who they really are, and they have no real empathy for others. Posing as a humanitarian, an intellectual, a church member, an honest businessman or woman, etc. gives them the cover story they need. It creates a narrative for who they want people to think they are.

Sharon L. Johnson

False Prophet

Jesus warned his followers, "Watch out for false prophets. They come to you in sheep's clothing, but inwardly they are ferocious wolves. Not everyone says to me, Lord, Lord, will enter the kingdom of heaven, but only he who does the will of my Father Who is in heaven."

A Christian narcissist is a false prophet. Many will say to me on that day, Lord, Lord, did we not prophesy in your name, and in your name drive out demons and perform many miracles? Then I will tell them plainly, I never knew you. Away from me, you evildoers!" (Matthew 7:15, 21-23) "For false Christs and false prophets will appear and perform great signs and miracles to deceive even the elect if that were possible. See, I have told you ahead of time." (Matthew 24:24-25)

These few verses tell us false prophets can: (a) Be gifted and talented people who deceitfully use the name and gospel of Jesus for recognition, power and/or money; (b) Perform great signs and miracles because they are associated with demons; (c) Have no affiliation with Christ and His gospel even though they may speak volumes about Jesus and salvation and (d) Will exist until the end of time.

In the book of revelation, a time is coming when the devil himself will call fire down out of the sky to prove that he is God, and this overwhelming miracle will deceive most of the inhabitants on earth. (Rev 13:13-14)

2 Timothy 3:1-7 gives you the characteristics and describes a Christian narcissist/false prophet for you. Here are some additional characteristics that go hand in hand on a Christian narcissist/false prophet:

- Very selfish people, it's only about them
- They constantly reference their own achievements, they love to self-promote to flaunt anything they believe might bring them praise "Not to seek our own glory and to let our work stand on its own (Proverbs 27:2)
- Emotional abusers
- They invade conversations under the guise of "helping" or "correcting" you, but they have no real interest in two-way dialog because they crave control, and their highest authority is always their own self-reference. "These people are grumblers and fault-finders; they follow their own evil desires; they boast about themselves and flatter others for their own advantage." (Jude 1:16)

- They twist scriptures. A Christian narcissist uses the scripture as a tool for their purpose instead of God's. They approach the Bible with a closed mind, memorizing verses to justify their behavior. The scriptures that conflict with their actions are ignored. "They are ungodly people, who pervert the grace of our God into a license for immorality and deny Jesus Christ our only Sovereign and Lord." (Jude 1:4)
- They put God second because they are selfish, and they love themselves first. We can only love God if we're unselfish. "Love the Lord your God with all your heart and with all your soul and with all your mind." This is the first and greatest commandment. (Matthew 22:37)
- They do not seek change because they feel as if there is nothing wrong with them
- Will flatter you all day, but if you cross them, they will retaliate and try and cause harm to whatever you love and value the most, excluding themselves—ministry, character. They are extremely dangerous people.
- Very subtle and sneaky with their abuse

- Very prideful and arrogant
- They blame their victim for everything
- Pathological liars who are really good at lying
- Sick on themselves very self-absorbed needs a lot of attention
- Inflated self-esteem
- Believe they are superior to others
- No empathy they can drum it up
- They pretend to have a big heart of God
- They appear to be sweet and caring
- Very controlling and manipulative
- When you are attached to them, they will sing your praises and become your number one fan
- They are very needy emotionally
- They do not respect or regard you or your boundaries
- They will use anger, the silent treatment, pouting, they will withhold affection, and disappear on you as a part of their emotional and mental abuse towards you
- Accuser of the brethren with a serpent tongue to flatter you and they use their tongue to scandal or

slander you
- They are envious of you. Jealousy is cruel as the grave and will kill your reputation and your ministry
- They are very smothering and can take over your life
- They are over the top. Because it is always about them, they must control their world
- They are very pushy and will not relent
- They have a Jekyll and Hyde spirit. They can be generous and kind, then they can be mean and hateful (public face/private face)
- Emotional. They will cry up a river to try and move you or make you believe their lies with their tears
- They do not know how to love
- They are always the victim

"Don't be naïve. There are difficult times ahead. As the end approaches, people are going to be self-absorbed, money-hungry, self-promoting, stuck-up, profane, contemptuos of parents, crude, coarse, dog-eat-dog, unbending, slanderers, impulsively wild, savage, cynical, treacherous, ruthless, bloated windbags, addicted to lust, and allergic to God. They'll make a show of religion, but behind the scenes they're animals. Stay clear of these people." (2 Timothy 3:1-3 (MSG)

"These are the kind of people who smooth-talk themselves into the homes of unstable and needy women and take advantage of them; women who, depressed by their sinfulness, take up with every new religious fad that calls itself truth. They get exploited every time and never really learn. These men are frauds who are twisted in their thinking, defying truth itself." (2 Timothy 3:6-9) (MSG)

Pastor R. C. Blakes stated in one of his teachings that narcissistic abuse is emotional abuse, and its intent is not to impact the moment, the intention of the emotional abuser is to strangle your future. He also stated the plan is an attack on your soul to break the soul. When a person's soul has been broken, they are divorced from themselves, and they are strangling their own future. He also gave a few signs of how to know if your soul has been broken.

- When you can't move on
- When you keep talking about your negative past
- When you can't make progress in your vision
- Accomplishing a great deal (overachiever) but you are not happy

A healthy soul lives forward, learns from the past, applies it and moves forward in the future.

Please Hear My Cry

Healing of a broken soul begins at the time of exposure. "Transparency is freedom." (Pastor R. C. Blakes)

Satan's Plots Against Godly Covenants

Many within the church, are seeking and desiring to be in godly relationships and covenants, because that is God's plan for our lives. But because of the level of desperation for Godly companionship, it becomes easy to let your spiritual guards down and hard to miss the foolish games that satan will play on you because of your gullibility. Can I tell you something? Just like you may be looking and seeking in the church for your covenant partner, satan is also looking and seeking for his next covenant partner in the church. Be mindful, that everyone that comes to church, doesn't love the Lord neither do they want to serve him. "Be alert and of sober mind. Your enemy the devil prowls around like a roaring lion looking for someone to devour." (1 Peter 5:8) (NIV)

Satan is attacking Godly covenants, so if he can come into our churches masked up as a believer, purposely set up and deceive the very elect; to cause them to attach themselves to the wrong covenant partner within the church, we have opened the door and given the enemy quite a bit of ground to start and complete his demonic assignment over our covenants, over our identities and over our destinies; right within the church. His assignment is to kill, steal and destroy God's sons and daughters.

But God does warns us in the last days that "false christs and false prophets will arise and perform great signs and wonders, so as to lead astray, if possible, even the elect." (Matthew 24:24) (KJV). He also tells us to watch out for false prophets as they will come to you in sheep's clothing, but inwardly they are ferocious wolves. They will come very well packaged on the outside. They will be gifted, well versed in the Word of God and talented people who deceitfully use the name and gospel of Jesus for recognition, power, and/or money purposes only. They will also perform great signs and miracles, they will speak volumes about Jesus and salvation, although they will have no relationship with Christ at all. Their whole goal is to walk in the spirit of full blown deception within the church; as they try to deceive as many of God's sons and daughters as possible; even in their Godly covenants.

The Aftermath

When a Christian narcissist realizes you recognize who they really are behind that fake mask, you immediately become their enemy. Why? Because they don't want you to expose them. In their head and eyes, that's a line you have crossed with them.

Let's talk a little about what character is, how important it is, and then talk about how the Christian narcissist manifests. What is character? It is what defines you. It is who you are. It's something you hold fast to inside, and how people see you on the outside. More importantly, it is something God always sees in you. It is one of the most important things you have. "A good name is rather to be chosen than great riches, and loving favor rather than silver and gold." (Proverbs 22:1)

Now being a studier of the word, Deacon Todd knew what the word says about the importance of character and protecting it. Immediately after our marriage chapter closed, he tried to destroy my name, integrity, and credibility by telling many lies about me to family, community, and friends. "When they would come to see me, they would speak falsely, while his heart gathers slander, then he goes out and spreads it around." (Psalms 41:6)

I immediately became his enemy when I saw who he really was underneath his mask. He feared I would expose him. Christian narcissists work really hard at maintaining their false image, and they fight really hard to keep it. When you become their enemy: They are the true definition of the accuser of the brethren. They will use their tongue to try and scandal or slander your name and deface your character. They will try and harm you and retaliate by trying to destroy anything or anyone you are in friendships with or associated within the ministry, on the job, in the community, even within the family or just anyone who has any level of respect for you and your character. "...ever secretly slanders his neighbor, him I will destroy. No one who has a haughty look and an arrogant heart will I endure..." (Psalm 101:5) I experienced all these things with Deacon Todd. He even took it to another level by telling people he didn't think I was saved anymore. He said I had walked away from God and there was something mentally not right with me. Those were the most absurd things that I had ever heard, and there is totally no truth in any of the lies he had spread about me. As I thought about it, I got chills because it was so destructive, demonic and sinister.

In my hometown, "not his" many people walked away from me, they agreed and believed the lies and circulated the lies for him. They snubbed me and didn't want to be bothered with me anymore. Many relationships and friendships ended. Even the people I thought were close to me seem to turn away and shut down. "But I say unto you, love your enemies, bless them who curse you, do good to them who hate you, and pray for them which despitefully use you and persecute you..." (Matthew 5:44) (KJV). The sad thing about all this was these were people who only saw the real love of God manifesting in me towards them. I genuinely loved them and I still do. I worked alongside them in ministry, mentored, counseled, imparted into, prayed and fasted for. I met with some late nights and talked on the phone with them when they were going through their valley seasons. I worshipped, fellowshipped, and worked in the community with them. "Many had become my enemies without cause; those who hate me without reason are numerous. Those who repay my good with evil, lodge accusations against me, though I seek only to do what is good." (Psalms 38:19-20) (KJV). It was if the very same people who I loved on and ministered to weren't giving me the benefit of the doubt. Their actions showed me they assumed the worst from this situation and my name had perished and no longer existed. "Mine enemies speak evil of me, when shall he die, and his name perish?" (Psalm 41:5) (KJV)

This was so hurtful, and this battle was way too big for me to fight. I heard God tell me to stand still and let him fight this battle for me. So that is what I did. I stood still, gave it to God, and allowed him to fight for me. "The Lord shall fight for you, and ye shall hold your peace." (Exodus 14:14) (KJV) I prayed and stood on the Word of God. It was hard to stay focused because people brought things about my ex to me, assuming they were helping me. But it would only feel like another dagger being pushed in my back. I also had so-called friends who appeared to have no empathy. Apparently, they just felt because Deacon Todd and I were Christians, we should have been able to work it out. Many lies were told about me to the place where it had people asking me, "Why wasn't I saying anything about what was being said about me?" First, God definitely had me hidden to the place that I didn't know about any of the lies being told. No one came directly to me. Secondly, why would I run around the city chasing lies and trying to correct them when they were just that, all lies. "Not a word from their mouth can be trusted; their heart is filled with malice. Their throat is an open grave, with their tongues they tell lies." (Psalm 5:9). (NIV) "Things hated by the Lord haughty eyes, a lying tongue, hands that shed innocent blood, a heart that devises wicked schemes, feet that are quick to rush into evil, a false witness who pours out lies and a person who stirs up conflict in the community." (Proverbs 6:16-19) (NIV).

The Lord surely had me and was protecting every part of my life during that time. My mind, my heart, my character, my image, my name. "The Lord will keep you from all evil; he will keep your life..." (Psalm 121:7). (ESV). I learned there are times in our lives when we must choose which battles we are to fight. "Do not retaliate with evil, regardless of the evil brought against you. Try to do what is good and right and honorable as agreed upon by all people if it is within your power, make peace with all people. Again, my loved ones do not seek revenge; instead, allow God's wrath to make sure justice is served. Turn it over to him, "Revenge is Mine. I will settle all scores." (Romans 12:17-20) (VOICE)

Why, why, why? He was my husband of 35 years. These are people I worked alongside in ministry and in life? Why did they hate and treat me as if they wanted me dead also? I had so many questions behind this, and it felt like sharp, fiery daggers being shot at me to make sure I was dead after the closing of my marriage chapter. These daggers were coming from all the people I thought loved, respected, and cared for me with the love of Christ? But there was one main question I would have asked if someone would have come directly to me "Why didn't you have my back and speak up for me when they were telling the lies on me or were you quiet?"

I did have someone come to me that was a friend to both of us, and we spoke on it a little but they took the position as if I wanted them to be on my side and they didn't want to take sides. They were gravely mistaken I didn't need them to take my side because I had God on my side and He is the only person I needed to be on my side. But it did allow me to see that individual's integrity, and who they really were and if they were going to stand up for wrong or righteousness. In the Kingdom of God, when did we start remaining neutral and not standing up or against right or wrong? "They say that what is right is wrong and what is wrong is right; that black is white and white is black, bitter is sweet and sweet is bitter..." Isaiah 5:20 (TLB)

I began asking the Lord many questions. What did I do wrong to anyone to be receiving so much hatred and hurt from people I genuinely love? Why did he go after my character? Why did he tell so many lies on me knowing I wasn't around to correct him? God answered although it wasn't the answer I wanted to hear. He said to me, I'm hiding and protecting you because this battle is not yours." He instructed me to submit to his process and trust him!!! I'm also testing your character to see how you are going to respond. Will you love me, or will you retaliate? I am preparing you for my use, and I want to see what is in your heart. We can fool men many times with our character, but you can't fool God. He sees our hearts and knows our intentions. "The eyes of the Lord are in every place, beholding the evil and the good." (Proverbs 15:3) (KJV)

Then there was the season, where I went through so much hurt. Church hurt, leadership hurt, family hurt, community hurt, and relational hurt. "I am worn out from sobbing. All night I flood my bed with weeping, drenching it with my tears. My vision is blurred by grief; my eyes are worn out because of all my enemies." (Psalm 6:6-7). (NLT) I didn't understand, so I ask the Lord, "Why so much hurt and pain from the ones I only showed Your love and compassion to? What do You need for me to learn from this?"

Have you ever had seasons in your life where there's no rhyme or reason about anything happening to you in the natural? You know God has His hands on you and is in it, so He must be up to something spiritually in your life. It may sound crazy, but from all the hurt I received, God taught me how not to treat His people. He taught me how to love my enemies, love the unlovable, how to treat and forgive the unforgivable, and expect nothing in return. "But love your enemies, do good to them, and lend to them without expecting to get anything back. Then your reward will be great, and you will be children of the Most High, because he is kind to the ungrateful and wicked. Be merciful, just as your Father is merciful." (Luke 6:35 -42) (NIV)

Demonic Warfare - It's A Family Thing

Years were passing, and our family was not in a good place spiritually. We were looking for direction from Deacon Todd, but no guidance was being given because he wasn't hearing anything from God. I unknowingly put demands on Deacon Todd because of where I thought he was spiritually; however, he did not know how or could not deliver on them. At that time, God had fully shown me the complete Deacon Todd. Our family was in a season where one minute we were in a thriving church and growing, and the next minute we are being locked out of that church with no place to go and no direction from our head. I didn't realize I was putting expectations on a person who wasn't who he was pretending to be. He was just going through the motions because it looked good in front of the people. Oh wow, how selfish! "Having the form of Godliness but denying the power within."

I was concerned about how a complete family just stopped moving forward because we were praying and waiting on our head, our covering. I looked to him as a wife should and tried to be a help meet for him during that time.

The more I tried to support and encourage him, it seemed to intimidate and make him jealous and angry. He would flip what I said and tell me I was not submitting, and letting him be the head!

Because of his insecurities, hurts, and things he was dealing with that he chose not to own up to and get some help, it was starting to affect his entire family and not just him. My daughters were having dreams about their dad taking the lead, but he did not to take the lead and leave our hometown. As a family, we were at a standstill, and we began to scatter so we could live, and not die spiritually. He wanted to go back to the religious church we left. There he could hide and continue to be who he was not, while his family spiritually died. We pleaded with him about our needs, but it just fell on death ears. It was very apparent that he wasn't concerned about his entire family unit, only himself.

On top of that, although Deacon Todd was home, he had already checked out mentally. His mother and brother were on their death and sick beds at the same time, and Deacon Todd spent more time with them than us. When he would come home, I tried to talk about different things going on in our family and what God was showing or saying, but he looked very lost. It was as though I was talking to a blank wall, or he didn't understand the words coming out of my mouth. God was showing me slowly, just where Deacon Todd was. He began to really change, and it was if I had become his enemy. We had confrontations and arguments when he was home. It was as if satan had told him I was finding out who he was, and he didn't like that. Earlier, I mentioned that he enjoyed it when I was underneath him because it made him feel as if he was in control.

He totally consumed himself with his mother and brother's illnesses rather than his family's spiritual illnesses. It was apparent, where his heart was, and it was not with his wife and children. Soon after, our house went into foreclosure from bad decisions he made about taxes. Now we were homeless, while he walked around as the savior of his family, community, and the church. When he made bad decisions that impacted our entire family, then he wanted to include me so I could be blamed for something he did.

Manifestation Time
The Real Deal

But as things began to really unfold towards the end of our covenant, Deacon Todd started telling me how he really felt about me. We all know satan is stupid, he is the father of all lies, and the accuser of the brethren, right? Well, Deacon Todd began to tell me how he felt I was jealous of him, and that I was competing against him in ministry. I was shocked and hurt at the same time. I responded and told him we were one, so why would I want to compete against my own husband and be jealous of him if we were one? It made no sense at all, but the Holy Spirit began to speak and let me know those demonic spirits in him were telling on themselves. I heard, "What he is accusing you of is how "he" really was and how he felt." A narcissist does this, and it is called projecting. They blame you for doing what they're doing or planning on doing. "Love is patient and kind. Love is not jealous or boastful or proud. (1 Corinthians 13:4) (NLT)

I had become my husband's enemy, and he was fighting against me. All I ever tried to do was support him and be there for him throughout the entire marriage and in ministry. Deacon Todd started to make me feel, and treat me as if I was a random woman on the street. Already having been betrayed because of his infidelity, now his words had become so cold and harsh toward me that it left me feeling hopelessly wounded. The shock of it all rocked my faith some but didn't destroy it. Our marriage had become mundane and was spiraling downhill fast. He had found other victims. The Christian narcissists search, find and fill their supply of victims through infidelity, unfaithfulness, and cheating with other people.

I prayed and asked God for the marriage and to allow my ex to have a real God experience. My ex didn't feel as if there was anything wrong with him, and he didn't have a desire to let God change him to save our marriage. We all know God will not go against anyone's will. Love never gives up, never loses faith, is always hopeful, and endures through every circumstance." (1 Corinthians 13:4-7) (NLT)

By this time, Deacon Todd had been walking in full-blown deception and unfaithfulness in our marriage for quite a while. I began to get closer and more intimate with God, and those spirits within him didn't like that at all. This is when the real person manifested, and it became scary for me naturally and spiritually. It seemed clear he was on an actual assignment in my life, and it was sinister. The intent was to kill, steal, and destroy any and all the faith I had, plus everything that resembled God and His light in my life.

It was evident I had allowed myself to become entangled with someone who really didn't fear God and wasn't in love with me or the God I loved. I had allowed myself to become entangled with someone who "I" believed was the one I was supposed to walk out destiny with, and not to the one who was a destiny stealer/killer.

It was like he had a love stronghold on me, and I was in a trance or a lost state of mind that was not my own. I looked at dysfunctional choices, words, and actions from him in our relationship as if it were okay. I would even find myself trying to fight or stand up for him on things other people saw as blatantly wrong. I couldn't see it because of the brainwashing I was under. It was so crazy. Now that I'm out of it, I can see it so clearly. It was very demonic. Mentally and emotionally, it played on my mind, which only added to the dysfunction. I had become so consumed and lost in the marriage, and all the fake love and dysfunction that came with his lies, manipulation, and control. It had me accepting and looking at the fake love as if it was real love.

Really, it was just the opposite. It was all abuse in different ways, just wrapped up in his toxic definition of love.

He continually lied to me about his whereabouts. There was the rejection in the bedroom and abandonment in our home, but on the outside, we had a God-fearing home. Although he was physically present, mentally, he wasn't there. He loved confrontation. He loved to downplay me as part of tearing down my self-esteem down to keep me under him. He loved to blame me for everything wrong in the marriage, and he never owned up to any of his faults. "Love does not demand its own way. It is not irritable, and it keeps no record of being wronged. It does not rejoice about injustice but rejoices whenever the truth wins out." (1 Corinthians 13:5-6) (NLT)

Over the years, our marriage continued to spiral downhill. There were confrontations and arguments, and sex wasn't enjoyable anymore. It felt like a duty to me. We would spend time together, but we were either fighting, or it was just plain boring. The love, fire, and connection in the covenant and the fight for the covenant that was there in the beginning, wasn't there anymore. Deacon Todd had allowed constant infidelity, lust, and pride to overtake him and his covenant. Yet he still walked around with his Christian mask on, his title, and with his Bible in his hand.

We were in an incredibly low place by this time in our covenant and "distant from each other," was very common in our home. Along with being very dysfunctional in a Christian home, our foundation was always cracked from the beginning, but it was just now manifesting years later. It was so bad, I thought we were unequally yoked after all these years. The things Deacon Todd really loved, was interested in, and had compassion for were not things of God. "Don't love the world, neither the things that are in the world. If anyone loves the world, the Father's love isn't in him." (1 John 2:15). (WEB) But the things I loved and was interested in were things of God. Which automatically caused us to be divided in the same house. "And if a house be divided against itself, that house cannot stand." (Mark 3:25). (KJV) Our already cracked foundation had began to crumble.

Consequently, it was like entertaining a perfect stranger who I never knew, even though this man would hold me and whisper sweet nothings in my ear every night. This is where God showed me what I was dealing with, and it wasn't flesh and blood, but this thing was spiritual. The man who slept with me and pretended in the beginning to have my back had allowed satan to enter and use him to work against me as if I was an enemy. "Then satan entered Judas, called Iscariot, one of the Twelve, and he went to the leading priests and captains of the Temple guard to discuss the best way to betray Jesus to them." (Luke 22:3-4) (NLT). I was in a betrayal season with the man I shared my bed with. The warfare was real, and it began to pull and drain my spirit. The Lord taught me how to fight in the spirit, to save my own life from my covenant partner. This spiritual fight kept me on my knees in prayer and caused me to be very aware of my surroundings while keeping my spiritual ears and eyes open at all times, even while sleeping. It was draining to know that I was sleeping and living with the enemy.

Deacon Todd stated that he didn't have a problem with women. I never told him, but the enemy tells on itself. Although Deacon Todd told on himself, he was in full-blown denial and did not want to own any of it or get the help he needed to save his covenant.

At this point, I didn't know what direction to go, so I went to God in prayer and asked for his direction. All I knew at that time, was that I loved the Lord and I just wanted to be in his will and to serve him; while who I was in covenant with chose to continue his lifestyle of sin. What I love about God is that he loves when we acknowledge and ask him for direction in our situations, he will do just that and turn your situation around, immediately!

All these years, Deacon Todd walked around masked as a Christian, teacher, preacher, deacon, God-fearing husband, and father on the outside while living another lifestyle. I had unknowingly yoked or allowed myself to become yoked with an unbeliever. "Do not become unequally yoked together with unbelievers. For what partnership have righteousness and lawlessness? Or what fellowship has light with darkness?" (2 Corinthians 6:14) (BLB). Once Deacon Todd knew I saw who he really was, what he was doing to me, and I didn't believe any more of his lies, that's when I really became his enemy. It was as if he didn't know me, or that we had been married for 35 years. He became confrontational and evil toward me, and I was afraid he would physically hurt me. "Love always protects, always trust, always hopes, always perseveres." (1 Corinthians 13:7) (NIV)

Deacon Todd had been exposed, and more exposure was going to come out. The real Deacon Todd came into full manifestation because none of his lies worked anymore. The nice side of him had totally disappeared; all I saw was the evil side of him.

As the marriage continued to spiral downhill, I was treated like his used property. Now, he had no use, need, or desire for me after 35 years. He used me as much as he could, and now it was just over. He found another supply to treat like his property to abuse and misuse them like he did me. He was still wearing the mask of a believer with a title who was well versed in the Word of God, but so demonic and sinister.

God's Will Be Done

I could see things in the covenant clearly starting to be shut down. The house was in foreclosure under his watch, there was no stability, no direction, and no concern or compassion for his covenant and family. Everything that seemed good about what we use to have was crumbling to a close. At that point, I began to seek God for His will to be done in my life, for His direction on my next move, and what I should do next. Our marriage had become really strained, and no one really knew the truth about our situation. All people knew were the lies he was sharing with his "yes" and carnal community. We went to counseling, but that didn't work. The marriage continued to spiral. I prayed, and I reached out to his so-called friends to help make him accountable. It became even worse, and I became fearful. I sought God and followed His direction to remove myself from the house. I moved up the street from where we were staying and rented an apartment for six months. Deacon Todd knew where I was staying and would come to visit as we were trying to work on reconciling. It was very apparent no one knew about our separation because people stopped me and asked, "Do you live out of town now?" To my surprise, when I said no, they would say, "Your husband said you had moved." It was if he was already trying to plot his story so people would see him as the victim, and I was the villain if the marriage failed. Of course, that was not the case at all. Why would Deacon Todd lie to people by telling them I had abandoned him? And then lie further by saying I moved out of town when I was living up the street from him? He was coming to see me, and we were working toward reconciling.

After the six months of talking, I believed we were moving forward. I moved back into the house, and it seemed all was well. But, the real person began to manifest again at another extreme level. More confrontation and arguing escalated to a higher level too.

Again, I sought God for direction as things got even worse. It began to take a toll on me. I was getting tired and feeling drained emotionally, mentally, and spiritually by all of it. His anger toward me was turned up, and again I felt extremely fearful that he would physically hurt me. It was if he was on a mission to force me to leave him and try and smear my name and character in the process. I saw it as a plan to make himself look like the victim, and I was the abuser when, in reality, he was silently abusing me.

I continued to seek the Lord for direction. He gave me clear instructions of transitioning me to a new place, which would remove me from the area with all my past hurts to a new place where my healing could begin. Then God could prepare me for His use.

At the time, my church was in Chicago. I made my first visit to look for a home closer to my church. God began to put it together for me and placed the right people in my path to help me with the transition. He gave me complete peace about everything going on in my life in that season. All my life, Peoria was the only city I had ever lived in. I knew God had gone before me because everything was connecting so well.

He placed me in Woodridge, Illinois, which I had never heard of, and didn't even know existed. It was only 35 minutes from my church in the city. It felt like home. Although I knew no one there, I knew God orchestrated my steps, and He was there with me and for me. I didn't realize everything that went into transitioning to a new city. God did, and He had me! God put together things for me financially, etc. and gave me nothing but pure peace.

As I moved from Peoria, God instructed me not to take anything because He would give me everything new. I took a couple things, bins with my clothes in it, and an air mattress to sleep on. It was a faith move and I believed God! I took the step, and I am so glad I did! Where would I be, if I had not been strong enough and to have faith in God to do what He instructed me to do. I could have been dead and six feet under because I couldn't deal with all the silent abuse I was under or in a crazy home. With all the manipulation and control, illness was racking my body because of the infidelity that defiled my bed.

As time passed and as I sought God for his direction, instruction, and moves concerning his will for my life. However, reconciliation with Deacon Todd was farther away because of his constant accusations and finger-pointing towards me about why our covenant didn't work. He didn't own his wrong; he just wanted to blame everything on me. This went on for a little while, and then the chapter was closed.

When the chapter was closed, and the Lord released me, Deacon Todd became very angry. He had lost his Godly marriage, and his ego took a big hit. The fake Godly image was at risk of being exposed to the church, community, and family. Deacon Todd lost control of everything. He saw nothing but blood and me as an enemy, and that immediately prompted more accusations.

He began to spew more lies. It was prophesied to me that curses were being spewed over me also. Sadly, it appeared as if the people I had a close relationship with, especially the people of God, believed him and his lies about me. "The Lord detests lying lips, but he delights in people who are trustworthy." (Proverbs 12:22) (NIV) "Their throats are open graves; their tongues practice deceit." "The poison of vipers is on their lips." "Their mouths are full of cursing and bitterness." "Their feet are swift to shed blood; ruin and misery mark their ways, and the way of peace they do not know." "There is no fear of God before their eyes." (Romans 3:13-18) (NIV)

He lied to everyone he thought had some respect for me, liked me, or knew me. He lied, cried and told family and friends he wanted his marriage, although he was still messing around with three of his young mistresses. If he wanted the marriage, he would have stopped all that messing around and worked on what I thought we had. But it was an act he played out to people to convince them once again that he was an innocent victim. All his lies were below the belt like when he told people he didn't know if I loved the Lord anymore. He tried to deface me, my character, and my credibility as he told people something was mentally wrong with me. The sad and demonic part about all this was that no one came to me and asked if any of it was true. After a couple of years passed, someone told me what Deacon Todd was saying about me. Many people in the city and church treated me and acted as if they believed him. These were the very same people I mentored, met with late at night and listen to their problems, counseled, cried, prayed with, fasted with, loved on, and spoke into. All they ever saw and heard from my lifestyle was the love of God towards them and for them.

I ask God many questions like, why so many enemies? What did I do? Was anyone a real friend? As I ask the question, God was giving me my answer at the same time. It was time to end many relationships within the community, church, city, and family. You say family too? Yes, family too. It was my trust season with the Lord because He was all I had, and He was the only one who could make sense out of all of this.

God connected me with the right resources and gave me favor in the court, where I was able to file for divorce pro bono without a lawyer. When the divorce process began, Deacon Todd was angry and didn't want to sign because the wording included adultery. I changed it to irreconcilable differences, and he still tarried, but eventually signed the papers after being served.

No Support

I had no support group, although I continued to reach out to different ones or someone to talk to. But the ones I found took what we casually discussed and caused more warfare for me as they added it to the lies already being told to tear me down more. Consequently, I learned to just trust Jesus and Him alone.

Many people turned on me, and I didn't even know what I had done wrong to them. All I remember doing was loving them, mentoring them, crying with them and fasting and praying for them. I heard the Lord say to me that He had to open my eyes and show me who His people really were. He wanted me to see how they will smile in my face while stabbing me in my back. How they will fellowship and break bread with me but couldn't stand me at all. They would pretend to be my friend only to use me for what God has given me. My inner circle began to clear out quickly as people turned on me for no reason and walked away because of the lies they believed. They acted like they were glad to see me down and glad to be rid of me. Then God began to distant people from me and remove people from my life. These people were the ones I thought would have been there for me but weren't. God assured me who was for my good, who His people really were, and who was against me. My circle became exceedingly small. In fact, only one or two people where there when God allowed.

Like a whirlwind, everything seemed to be happening so quickly. As I write about it, I feel like I was purposely set up by God, where I had nowhere to go and no one to turn to, but Him. It was my TRUST season, and it was just God and me.

Desert Season

The dessert season was a very lonely season for me. It's a place where it seemed as if God was not there many times. But we know God is Jehovah-Shamaah, and He is always there. During that time, I had to learn how to totally submit to the potter's touch, perfectly, and unresisting (Jeremiah 18:6). The dessert is a beating and grinding place used for submission unto the potter's wheel and refining in the fire. "Behold, I have refined you, but not as silver, I have tested you in the furnace of affliction." (Isaiah 48:10) (KJV)

I had to learn one of life's strategic keys, which is to embrace what the Lord brings into our lives with thanksgiving. "In everything give thanks: for this is the will of God in Christ Jesus concerning you." (1 Thessalonians 5:18) (KJV) When I did, I recognized His sovereignty, control, and completely yielded myself to Him. He will never waste our sorrows. He turns them into precious jewels. He uses our suffering to birth beautiful new things into our lives.

Healing Process Begins

My healing process began when God transitioned me to a new city, and when I closed all points of contact with my abuser. In the beginning, while the covenant was ending, Deacon Todd contacted me. Our conversations started off well like we could try to reconcile. He said he still loved me and wanted to see the marriage work. But soon I would find out it was all lies and always turned into an argument in which he blamed me for everything. I felt like it was his goal to see me upset by throwing more hurtful daggers in my heart. If he could get me to argue with him, the self-gratification made him feel he still had control of my heart. I saw the pattern and that's when, in my studies, the Lord allowed me to read about having "no point of contact" with him. I changed my name and number and closed all the doors of communication and forms of contact. That ended all the manipulation, torment, and control he was still trying to use on me.

Think about this, if I left the doorways open for him to enter when he wanted or to contact me when he wanted, it wasn't giving me a chance to heal. I was giving him an open door to come in and out of my life to see if he still had my heart, and if I had feelings for him. He still wanted power and control of my life while he was moving on with his.

God began His masterwork of healing and putting the pieces of my broken heart back together again. He transformed and renewed my mind and thoughts with the Word of God. He began to gut me out and heal my soulish areas where I wanted to hold on to the past and retaliate for everything wrongfully done to me. God made it clear that my healing was going to come through letting go of the past and forgiving each person who purposely caused me pain and hurt throughout this entire process. He showed and taught me so many things about myself, and they were the good, the bad, and the ugly. God also showed and taught me more about His people and how not to treat them and how to love them unconditionally through my process. The people in the church, judged and treated me so badly and I didn't witness or experience very little, if any, of God's love in action towards me, at all. (Sigh)

That part of the process was not easy because it came with so much hurt from his people. But it was necessary and is how the genuine love of God was birthed in me as to how to treat His people with kindness, forgiveness, and how to love unconditionally.

After this season, I saw Deacon Todd a few times because of our children and grandchildren at life events like graduations, childbirth, etc. I thank God, that when I saw him, I was able to treat him with the love of God, I would say that I had forgiven him. But it wasn't until the Lord really started dealing with my heart and I got to the place where I started feeling sorry for him, that I knew I had genuinely really forgiven him.

Effect On The Children

Although our children were grown, they went through a season of trying to process everything that happened with the divorce of their mom and dad. There was hurt, manipulation, and confusion still going on from their dad. He wanted them on his side. Sides! Who creates sides? Certainly not adults, only children do that.

I understand our children loved us both, and they tried to support us. Although all I ever wanted them to do was to stand up for right and against wrong throughout the entire situation. I didn't want them to take sides because we were their parents. I was blamed for making them feel like they had to choose between the two of us because I was released and left the union. But I was tired and didn't want to be abused anymore by their dad.

1. It was apparent our children were hurt, blinded, and confused during that time. Although their words seemed as if they were standing up for right, their actions seemed to be in total agreement and support with their dad's abuse against me. "Woe to those who call evil good and good evil, put darkness for light and light for darkness" (Isaiah 5:20). (NIV) It

was as if I was the enemy because I was standing up for righteousness and what the Word says. It wasn't anger or bitterness toward their dad, it was just making a bold stand for holiness that caused division between my children and me. My position was so firm, they wanted to give me labels as if I was bitter toward their dad and as if I needed to get some help. The scripture Matthew 10:22 (KJV) came to mind, "And ye shall be hated of all men for my name's sake: but he who endureth to the end shall be saved."

They just wanted a relationship with their mom and dad. Obviously, they didn't understand their dad had made a conscious decision to live a life of sin, and I had chosen to live for Christ. That automatically caused us to be divided. We did not have teams, but we were divided because of our beliefs and our choice of lifestyles. (Read 2 Timothy 3). They still could have a relationship with both of us, but it could not be blended as it once was.

The sad part about it all is that all the children wanted was a relationship with their father as they remember him, seeing him go to churches and prisons to preach and teach. But that wasn't their father was anymore, although he still wore the mask of a Christian and went through the motions. "Having a form of godliness but denying its power" (2 Timothy 3:5). (NIV)

They didn't understand that to have a relationship with their father in his broken state would mean having a relationship and being in agreement with everything their father was doing, and to be okay with what was attached to their father who was not Christ-like. They were too afraid to confront him about his lifestyle because he was their father, and they felt he knew what he was doing with his life since he was grown.

There were many times when I was alone, and it appeared as if they were supporting the wrong more than they were supporting the right. "Woe to those who call evil good and good evil, who put darkness for light and light for darkness, who put bitter for sweet and sweet for bitter!" (Isaiah 5:20). (NIV) It was if because they had been in dysfunction and saw wrong being done before them for so long, their actions and natural eyes blocked out the wrong they saw, and they were in total agreement with all the craziness going on. The sad part was when they would spend time with their father, they would come back acting like him.

Throughout the entire process, I never tried to keep them away from Deacon Todd. I only suggested that they give him some space, so he could get himself together spiritually. But of course, I was the enemy in their eyes, and they didn't see that I was just trying to protect them from some unnecessary hurt from their dad. All they saw was I didn't want them to be around him. (Sigh)

I prayed for my children that the blinders be taken off their eyes, so they could see their father. I prayed that the unhealthy soul ties and strongholds be destroyed between their father that kept them locked up in bondage, supporting his wrong and disfunction. I also prayed for their dad, that he received a real God experience and know Christ before it's too late.

Closing

How did I miss it, and why didn't I see him or these things early on? Why didn't I see his mask? Why did I believe all his lies? Why did I allow him to use and abuse me the way he did? If I was missing it, why didn't someone love me enough to tell me? Why did I allow him to manipulate and control me like he did? Why did I stay so long and allow that man to do so much to me that was hurting me and not helping me?

I've come to grips with reality. I was very young, naïve, and green behind the ears. I was a good church girl, and I didn't know anything about the world for real. I didn't realize some very evil people in the world are broken and hurting and want to break and hurt people just like them. I never should have allowed Deacon Todd to connect with me. But he saw that as an excellent opportunity and chose me as his next victim of abuse to manipulate, control, and use while he called it love.

Because of the way he came packaged, the way he spoke, and promised all kinds of things to me and the way he was wrapped all up nicely with so many smooth empty and deceptive promises, I believed him. But he deceived me to the point where I really believed he was the one for me, and I was the one for him.

When a person is or has been in a relationship with a Christian narcissist, masked non-believer, and false prophet because of all the deception, control and manipulation being used against them, trying to tell the story or explain what they came out of will not be understood by everyone. Others saw the nice side of the man I was in covenant with, but they never saw the evil side of him, only I did.

When you are in it, the enemy has you blinded to make you feel and see it all in the name of love. Just so you know, love from your partner should never blind or hurt you.

Why do we as women deem it to be okay to accept silent abuse from individuals that say they love us? But do intentional things to us; to keep us down and tear down our self-esteem to make us doubt our own self-worth.

But that was one question I was able to look my abuser in the face and ask him, "If you weren't in love with me, why didn't you just say so? I could have moved on with my life." He never answered; he only had a blank look on his face.

Encouragement

If you offer your heart to someone who is not on your level, you can compromise your destiny.

Life situations do not dictate or determine who that person is. That was just a part of that person's process, which qualifies them to walk in their real purpose.

What do I mean? God had me so protected, He did not allow me to hear about everything happening in my life that caused me hurt and pain. All my ugly scars came through long-term betrayal, deception, embarrassment, shame, hurt, and lies from companions and friends. God was protecting and guarding me for real.

Of course, I had a talk with my Father...and His response to me was..."I heard your prayer, and I am doing what you ask Me to do. Trust Me and know that I am God I know what's best for you, and I am working things out for your good. Despite what it looks or feels like, continue to go on the journey with Me as I take you to higher places."

Ever have a time in your life when bad things were coming at you back to back to back? I had a season where everything and people were being removed.

Have you ever experienced or went through things in your life that should have taken you out of here naturally and/or spiritually speaking? God will remove and allow you to step out of the situation to realize how He was protecting and keeping you during turmoil and harm that was all around you. His word is true when He says, "He will never leave us or forsake us." Look back and see God's amazing love for you while His hands were all on you, preventing harm and death from overtaking you. What an awesome God I serve!

Conclusion And Encouragement

With God's help, I have endured many years of misery, pain, and suffering in my Christian journey by the hands of His children, my lover, my husband, my covenant partner who stood before God and said, "I DO" "I WILL" "FOR BETTER OR WORSE" "I PROMISE TO TAKE CARE OF HER..." But only to hear my covenant partner tell his children at the end of this chapter, he didn't regret anything (betrayal, disrespect, unfaithfulness, control, manipulation, and financial abuse) that he had done in his life towards me. It totally left the already confused, emotionally drained, and broken me devastated. I believe we all have a Judas in our lives, and they know exactly what their assignment is and how long it will take to get it done. In the end, it was if he had manifested into who he really was and he was my assigned Judas. He knew exactly what his assignment was in my life and exactly when and how he was to complete it. It all seemed so sinister, cold-blooded, and demonically plotted out as if he didn't even know me after 35 years of marriage. But he knew his assignment and it was to try and stop me from fulfilling my purpose or either drain the life out of me.

I immediately thought to myself, OMG, all these years I wasted. He wasn't part of my destiny, and I wasn't even supposed to have been connected with him. So much of my precious time. I may have been shaken, but not sifted.

It didn't work!

In closing, I want to encourage my sisters and say if you have made choices in your life that connected you to the wrong one and unfortunately caused you to go through or still be in it, God is a loving and kind God. He sees and knows every decision we make, good or bad, and He sees everything we go through. He doesn't want to see His precious daughters silently suffering at the hand of a Christian narcissist or a person masked up as a Christian with demonic intent to waste His precious daughter's time. You cannot get time back while being held down or back from walking out purpose and destiny.

I shared my story to encourage and let my sisters know that despite whatever the enemy had set up to try and destroy you, that may have left you angry, damaged, bitter, broken, wounded, scarred, feeling lost, falling apart and feeling forgotten, know that God's not done with you. He has a plan for you, and He's still writing your story, and this was just a part of it. It's not over, it's only the beginning.

Please Hear My Cry

God is going to finish what He started in you. Don't give up, because God needs you and your story.

End Testimony

You are looking at God's impossible made possible. He brought me through public humiliation and shame, but I made it through. I experienced so much loss, hurt, rejection, shame, deception, betrayal, smearing of my character, and lies, but I made it through!

I could have lost my mind or been dead in my grave, or sickness, racking my body because of what was being brought to defile my bed, but I made it!

Yes, I have had to cry many tears, and I have many scars, but it has made me better, stronger, and wiser, and I made it through.

Despite it all, and many times I didn't understand it at all, but He still has a plan for my life, and it's working for my good.

God had me, and I know Him to be a sustainer, keeper, protector, friend, husband, and everything and anything I needed Him to be for me. He was just that!

I remember the story about Paul when he was in a storm on the boat, and then he was bitten by a venomous snake. This snake bite could have paralyzed him for life or could have just killed him instantly. But Paul was not afraid or shocked. He shook the snake off into the fire and suffered no harm.

As I am ending my story, I want to encourage my sisters and let them know that snake bites and assaults will happen in our lifetimes and will be sent from satan to try and stop you, paralyze or kill you. But because the enemy does not have authority over your life and destiny, it will not work.

I learned through my process, that if I stayed close to the fire (intimacy with God and experience visitations from God), I could gain authority over my snakes. But if you do not stay near the fire, assaults and snake bites will end you.

Prayer ... "Lord, I want to stay in the center of the flame."

Closing Remarks

I pray you don't ever allow yourself to be fooled, your heart to be snagged, and to settle down with a counterfeit person full of deception and lies who is allowing satan to use them to destroy you and your destiny.

Please know that God has a plan for your life, plans to prosper you and not to harm you, plans to give you hope and a future. It is crucial to know who God has sent for you to be connected and in covenant with, in order to walk out your Godly destinies together. Not that you desire because of how it might look to you with your natural eyes. Be not deceived. It could be a false delusion, a distraction sent from Hell, and wrapped up with love to try to steal, kill and destroy you and to steer you right out of the center of God's will and His plans for your life.

End Of The Story

I thought he had my back. I thought we were in love with each other. But he was the same person who abused me in many ways. In private, he tore down my self-esteem and endangered my health many times because of his unfaithful lifestyle. He disrespected me with habitual lies slandering my name and ministries all because of jealousy, envy, and pride.

A question for you, "ARE YOU IN COVENANT WITH THE RIGHT ONE?"

The choice of a spouse will have a significant effect on your life, physically, spiritually, and emotionally. I heard Bishop Dale C. Bonner, Senior Pastor of Word of Faith Family Worship Cathedral say in one of his Conferences, "Nothing sabotages a person's life mission quicker than being in covenant/relationship with the wrong one."

I now see all those things people did to me were only because they were trying to hold me back and to stop me from walking into my destiny. With God's help, I made it. I am an overcomer! This is my season and opportunity to allow God to rebuild what He truly wants in me, and for me to match His plans for my life. Yes, I had to start all over.

Now, I am living my best life because God orchestrates my steps, and I am sitting in the middle of His will as I walk out my purpose. What an awesome place to be!

www.ingramcontent.com/pod-product-compliance
Lightning Source LLC
Chambersburg PA
CBHW071608170426
43196CB00034B/2225